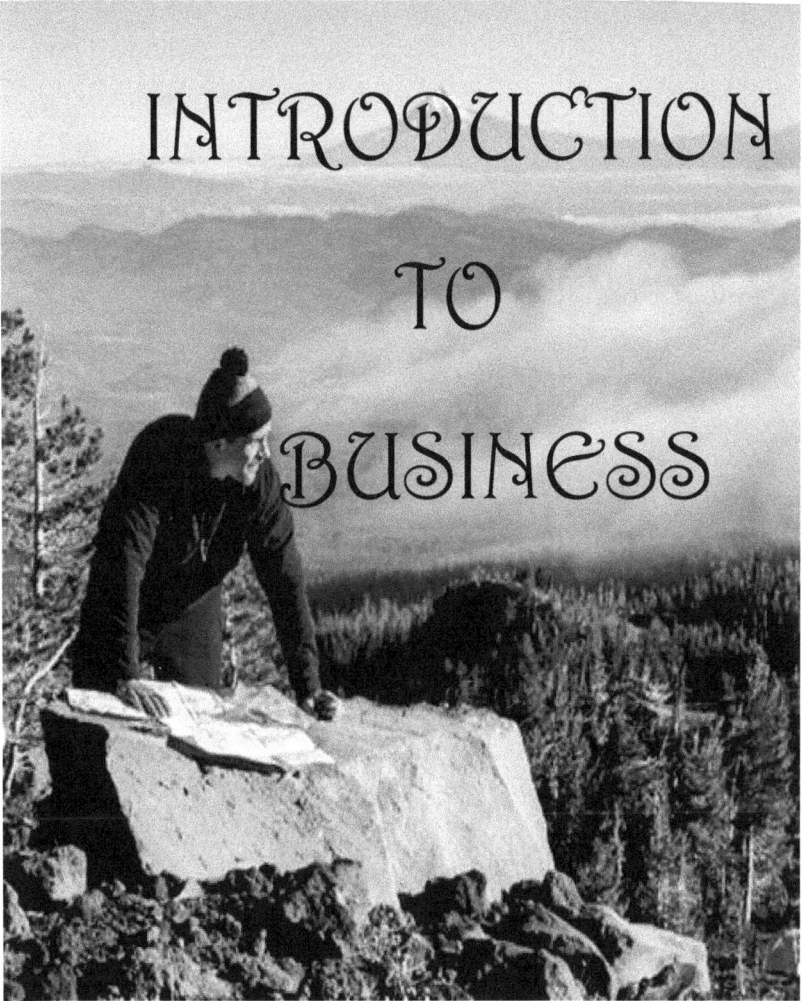

INTRODUCTION

TO

BUSINESS

INTRODUCTION

TO

BUSINESS

BY

PHILIP KUNLE AKIODE

(HND, MSc, AMNIM, MCIM, ACIS (Shipping), ACTI, ACA, ACFE)

For additional copies of this or other Philips Kunle Akiode titles write:

Korloki Publishing Company (A subsidiary of Allzents Groups Inc.)

P.O. Box 300605, Brooklyn, New York 11230

Please allow 4 to 6 weeks for delivery.

For bulk orders contact us via email @

Korloki@yahoo.com

Cover design by: Korloki Publishers, Inc.

Interior design: Korloki Publishing Company

Photographs: Google Clip Arts assembled by Korloki Graphic

Summary: A comprehensive business study book for students in colleges and undergraduates

ISBN 13: 978193739301

ISBN 10: 1936739305

PRINTED IN USA

DEDICATION

Akiode Foundation

FOREWORD

A casual observer of the business environment in Nigeria is quick to see a duality in respect of successful business lying side by side moribund ones. What is responsible for this? Are there fundamentals to business success? These are the questions that Akiode sets out to answer in this study manual. His approach is to prescribe a total package perspective comprising issues that are inherent to business and those that are outside business that impact significantly on business success; those that should be considered by business promoters if they are to make informed decisions. Also, emphasized are the interdependencies between what may be considered as predictors of business success in Nigeria.

Informed institutions such as the Nigeria Economic Summit Group, Chambers of Commerce and Industries, Manufacturers Association, Trade Unions etc. have attested to the high cost of doing business in Nigeria with many contributory factors including government policies summersault, poor infrastructure, lack of access to finance, dearth of managerial capacity, weak legal regime, poor work ethics etc.

This study manual is an excellent guide to all those who want to run successful business or who want to know how people run successful business using Nigeria as a case. The manual emphasizes on what to do to avoid business failure by identifying what could constitute obstacles to success and how to overcome them. In effect Akiode provides what may be considered the key success factors in doing business in Nigeria.

The manual began with the need to conduct a reality check i.e. to have a good understanding of what business is, who the business stakeholders are and the importance of developing appropriate value propositions to meet their expectations. It also emphasized the importance of distinguishing various forms of businesses, knowing their peculiarities, the different risks to which they may be prone and how the risks can be managed. The author recommends ab initio a thorough understanding of relevant sectors of the Nigerian business environment so as to guide investment decisions and promote efficient resource utilization.

He suggested a number of planning tools to aid in the systematic collection and analysis of data and cautioned on the importance of ensuring that plans are based on data that have integrity.

Drawing on his experience as a teacher to student of business and as a consultant to some entrepreneurs, the author is of the opinion that prime consideration must be given to understanding the role of government in promoting or discouraging business success through the availability or absence of an enabling environment (infrastructure, power, communication, transportation etc.). Such understanding should assist business promoters to make informed choices as to sector, product/services, location, and to be able to make reliable estimate of the cost of doing business in Nigeria.

Equally, they should know how those factors are changing (rate of change and direction of change) so as to predict their effects on business success. Finally, he suggests that ethics has an important role to play in doing business in Nigeria. A good understanding of the above fundamentals should enhance the probability of business success.Joseph Garba Donli Ph.D.

INTRODUCTION

TO

BUSINESS

A

STUDY MANUAL

BY

PHILIP AKIODE

(HND, MSc, AMNIM, MCIM, ACIS (Shipping), ACTI, ACA, ACFE, CFA Module 1)

January 2014

Chapter One

Definition and characteristics of business

1.0 Business: Definition, Purpose and Objective

1.1 What is Business?

There are various ways to define "business". For instance, Adeleke and Akiode define business as "any legal activity performed by man for the purpose of earning a living". This means that drivers, clerks, barbers, iron benders, pastors, pilots, factory workers, secretaries, builders, farmers, contractors, directors, governors, lawyers, accountants, architects, musicians, doctors, hairdressers, boxers, footballers, engineers, mechanics, teachers, hawkers, traders, etc. are all engaged in business. A lawyer is in the business of defending his clients, a barber is in the business of hair cutting, a doctor is in the business of healing, an accountant is in the business of keeping financial records and reporting same, etc. Whatever a person does to earn a living is his or her business.

There is however, one important factor, which distinguish business from other non-business activities and that is "it must be legal" i.e. it must not be against the law of the land. Several examples of illegal activities, which do not constitute business abound e.g. prostitution, smuggling, robbery, assassination, shoplifting, etc. You will agree that some people engage in the activities for their livelihood but because of their illegality, they do not qualify to be called business.

Keith and Gubellini say "a business is a person or group of persons properly organized, who produce or distribute goods and services with a view of profit". The view here is that business is an organized (or formal) set up with formal structures in place (i.e. properly organized). You will agree with me that this is not often the case. This definition holds only for permanent (as opposed to temporary) business ventures.

The Cassell Paperback Dictionary also defines business as:

1. Employment, occupation, trade, profession.

2. Serious occupation, work

3. Duty, concern

4. Commercial, industrial or professional affairs

5. Commercial activity

6. Buying and selling

7. A commercial establishment

8. A shop with stocks, etc.

Just as no man (or woman), country or group of people is self-sufficient, every business depends on other businesses for survival e.g. a manufacturer needs raw materials from other business ventures. So also must he depend on wholesalers and distributors to push his goods into the market?

Sometimes, we talk about the business of governance. This implies that governance is also a business and a serious one for that matter. If the government is not able to fulfil its responsibilities to the citizenry, there is a serious negative impact on the society. Some of the effects of bad governance (bad government business) include corruption, lack of or inefficient social amenities, inflation, armed robbery, unemployment, poverty and insecurity.

1.2   Purpose of Doing Business

People that go into business have but one purpose – to do something, which is useful to others and for which, they can afford to exchange their money. Thus, it could be to manufacture goods, buy and sell goods, provide or render services that are beneficial to others.

Anybody who aspires to do business must therefore evaluate his/her capacity to satisfy others before embarking on the venture. Satisfaction is what people actually pay for and any business that does not aim at achieving this is likely to fail in the medium and long term even though it succeeds in the short-term. Business succeeds only if the customers who are willing to patronize the business on a continuing basis pay for the goods/services provided/rendered. Business stops when patronage stops/ends. Every businessman/woman (or entrepreneur) must bear this in mind to be able to stay in business.

1.3   Objectives of Doing Business

No matter the size of type of any business, there is but one primary objective and that is "to make profit". Profit is the excess of revenue earned over the amount invested in the business. This objective is true of profit-making and non-profit making ventures. If we revalue the assets of a non-profit making organisation and there is a surplus over the amount invested, the profit objective is true. The only difference is that while the profit is shared/distributed/retained in a profit-making business, the profit is not even computed in the case of not-for-profit organizations, not to talk of sharing/distribution. Other business objectives could include the maximization of the wealth of its owners, expansion growth, diversification, social responsibility, etc.

1.4   Profit Making Versus Not-for-Profit Organizations

Perhaps, the main distinguishing factor between profit-making and non-profit-making organization is the objective for establishing these businesses or organizations. Whilst profit-making organisations expect financial reward (profit) from their investment(s), not-for-profit organisations do not profit but other things e.g. a political party aims to win an election by ensuring that more voter-members are recruited into the party. The success of a church or other religious organisations is measured in terms of number of new members/converts. Even when financial rewards accrue at the end of the day; these are not the main purpose/focus of establishing such organisations.

1.5   Characteristics of Business

The following are the features of business:

- Provision of product(s) or service(s) to satisfy human wants;

- Legality

- Utilisation of Resources

- Working towards an objective

- Investment

- Location

- Relationships

- Market

- Decision-Making

- Profit or Loss

- Risk/Uncertainty

These features are discussed below.

1.5.1 Provision of Product(s) or Service(s) to Satisfy Human Wants

The purpose of any business, as earlier mentioned, is to provide good(s) and/or service(s) that is/are capable of satisfying human wants. The product(s) may be small (e.g. pins, clips, buttons, etc); big e.g. (airplanes, vehicles, houses, etc); cheap (e.g. specialized drugs); technological (e.g. computers, space crafts, solar power equipment, etc.); or it may be a luxury (e.g. jewelries).

The service(s) may be any of the following: legal managerial, gardening, barbing, skincare, shoe shining, accounting, teaching, distribution (wholesaling/retailing) and a host of others.

1.5.2 Legality

Whether the business is for the provision of goods or for the rendering of services, the business done must not infringe on the laws of the land or on the rights of the citizenry (individual or corporate).

1.5.3 Utilization of Resources

Every business makes use of resources. These resources are usually referred to as the 5Ms of Men, Money, Machines, Materials, and Methods. The men are the various categories of workers engaged to assist the owner(s) with the day-to-day running of the business. The money represents both the fixed (long-term investment) and working capital of the business. Machines are the different types of equipment used in the business. Equipment is required whether the business is engaged in manufacturing or not, e.g. a barber needs clippers, a distributor needs delivery vans or bicycles, a tailor needs sewing machines, etc. Materials represent the raw materials that are deployed to manufacture the product(s) required by the business to satisfy human wants. Methods represent the various decisions and actions deployed by the owner of the business to achieve the purpose and objective(s) of setting up the business.

1.5.4 Investment

Every business involves investment. The investment is usually in terms of money or money's worth. Apart from money, other things that are usually invested in a business include land, building(s), knowledge, skill or expertise of the owner as well as time. All these must be invested and judiciously employed to achieve the purpose and objective(s) of the business in an efficient and effective manner.

1.5.5 Location

A business must have a location or an address for communication and contact. It could be an internet address or a post office box. What is important is that the business must be accessible i.e. it must be capable of being reached by its current and potential customers as well as other interested parties.

1.5.6 Relationships

A business must necessarily establish relationships with its employees/workers, customers, agents, government, etc. in some businesses, the better the relationship with its numerous publics; the easier it is to achieve its purpose and objective(s). For instance, a hostile relationship with workers or their union may affect the quality of product(s) or service delivery. This will in turn affect sales and consequently revenue and profit.

1.5.7 Market

Nobody establishes a business for the purpose of satisfying self. The business must serve a market. Sometimes, the market exists and sometimes, it must be created. The buyers of the product(s) or services sold by the business are its market. The market could be in a catchment area or widely dispersed.

1.5.8 Decision Making

This is an essential aspect of business. Whether the business is big or small, decision must be taken on how much capital is required, number and category of staff to be employed and how much their remuneration would be, where to locate the business, what to produce, how (i.e. method) to distribute the goods, market penetration/sustenance strategy, whether and when to expand, etc.

1.5.9 Profit or Loss

Although the objective of any business is to make profit, sometimes, transactions result in a loss because of prevailing economic, social, political, and other conditions/circumstances. Profits and Losses are therefore permanent features of business. The better a business is managed and the more favorable the operating environment, the more likely profitable the business would be and vice-versa.

1.5.10 Risk/Uncertainty

Risk and uncertainty are permanent features of a business. Uncertainty has to do with the inability to accurately predict the future business environment while risk is the chance (i.e. possibility) of loss or peril.

Chapter Two

The Nigerian Business Environment

2.0   Business and Environment

Business is never done in a vacuum. It is done within society, which is pluralistic in nature (i.e. composed of many organized groups with varying interests). Each of these groups exerts influence/power over the way business is conducted, the prices charged, the quality of products and services, etc. because of their divergent goals. For a business to run successfully and fulfil its purpose to society, it must integrate the interests of these various groups otherwise there will be incessant conflicts which will no doubt bring the business to an abrupt end.

The various groups and interests within a society in which a business operates are referred to as "environment". The societal/environmental groups may be many or few depending on the nature/type of business and the prevailing circumstances. They may include trade/workers' unions, chamber(s) of commerce, government(s), employers' associations, religious interests, consumer protection associations, tax payers, students, women associations, youth associations, etc. Every business must identify, evaluate and react/respond to the forces in the environment that may affect its operations.

The business environment can be broadly classified into two main groups – internal and external. The internal environment is generally considered to be controllable (i.e. can be easily manipulated by the businessman). The external environment on the other hand is largely uncontrollable and must be regularly evaluated and appropriate steps taken to take decisions that will enable the business to respond in the most appropriate manner. By so doing, the company will be able to manipulate its environment to achieve its desired purpose and objective.

The external environment of a business can be divided into four main groups:

Economic, social, political/legal and technological.

2.1   The Economic Environment

It is important to understand the economic environment in which a business operates. The economic environment relates to and influences the prices paid for various factor inputs into production, distribution, consumption, etc. A business must regularly evaluate the effect of the following on its operations: capital, labor, price levels, fiscal/tax policies and customers.

2.1.1   Capital

Since no business can be self-sufficient, additional capital must be sourced from the market. How much is available for that business in the short, medium and long term as well as the level of interest paid is a function of and is determined by the economic environment. Therefore, if a business must source additional capital (in excess of what it is capable of providing), it must examine critically the economic environment to determine which source is suitable for it at a price favorable to the continued operations, existence and survival of the business.

2.1.2   Labor

The amount, quality and price of labor are important determinants of the success of a business. Some of the evaluative questions which the business must ask and seek answers to include: is the right quality of labor available? If yes, is it available in the right/required number (for immediate and future need)? What is the price at which labor can be sourced (i.e. salaries and wages payable)? Can we afford to pay this price? If we pay this price, what is the effect on our operation, on the attainment of our purpose and profitability? What is the effect on the quantity and quality of our output of product(s) and/or services? etc. The answer to some of these questions explains why some businesses are established in locations where labor is cheap and in ample supply. In some societies, untrained (unskilled) labor is available in abundance while in others, only highly skilled and technical personnel may be available. The cost of labor (even unskilled labor) may be high in some other locations. All these must be studied and balanced by the businessman.

2.1.3 Price Levels/Inflation

A business acquires various inputs for its operations and this acquisition is shaped by the level and direction of changes in the price level as it affects the business. The situation may still be fairly comfortable and controllable if the price level changes are not rapid (i.e. only occasional). Where the price level changes are rapid leading to inflation, turbulence may result in the economic environment and the effect on both the input and output sides of the business can be severe. Inflation not only upsets business but also has highly disturbing influences as it affects the costs of labor, materials, capital, etc. and it may not be possible to pass the extra costs unto the consumers/buyers of the products and/or services offered by the business.

2.1.4   Fiscal and Tax Policies of Government

The nature of government fiscal and tax policies have serious economic impact on business. For instance, government's control of credit availability and price of credit through policy has considerable impact on business. In the same vein, the tax policy of the government affects every segment of the society, especially business ventures. For example, if the tax on business profit is very high, it may serve as a disincentive to go into business. The consequence of this is that investors will look elsewhere to invest their capital. If sales tax is imposed, prices will rise and people will reduce their purchases of the affected items.

2.1.5   Customers

The customers who patronize a business want as much value as possible for their money. Therefore, every business must consider this in their relationship with customers.

Apart from economic considerations, a host of other factors (which shall be discussed later affect the relationship between a business and its customers.

2.2   The Social Environment of Business

The social environment is made up of the attitudes, desires, expectations, degree of intelligence and education, beliefs and customs of the people in a given environment. A business must be socially responsible by considering the impact of their actions on society. We shall discuss two angles of the social environment of business, viz:

(a) The complexity of environmental forces

(b) Social attitudes, beliefs and values

2.2.1 The Complexity of Environmental Forces

Environmental elements are interwoven. This makes their study and comprehension exceptionally difficult. Forecasting them, anticipating and preparing for changes thus become more difficult. According to Weihrich and Koontz, social desires, expectations and pressures give rise to laws and standards of ethics. Social forces including ethics normally arise before laws are passed, since the legislative process is notable reactive in the sense that it acts when a crisis is at hand but seldom before. Furthermore, existing laws and regulations, which are so numerous and compiled that even the best-trained lawyers cannot know all of them (though they would probably know where to find them), often are brought to our attention in surprising and unusual ways.

2.2.2   Social Attitudes, Beliefs and Values

Attitudes, beliefs and values differ among workers, employers, the rich and the poor, students, entrepreneurs, etc. this makes it difficult for businessmen/women to design an environment conducive to performance and satisfaction. When these forces are external, they become more difficult to respond to. There is therefore, an uphill task for the business owner to appreciate the complexity of the social environment in which business is done and endeavor to respond appropriately. Business owners must realize the fact that when people's standard of living improves, their expectations for a better life tend to increase even faster.

The following report on the failure of managers to respond to changes in their environment is useful and relevant here for consideration/discussion.

"The need to review and renew the marketing concept is now urgent for the following reasons:

The failure of management in general and marketing management in particular to realize the seriousness of or to react quickly enough or constructively enough to the changes taking place in the environment.

Society is changing and demanding different standards of behaviour from companies towards the community and towards their employees – the young, the disabled and the older executives. Society expects more than it is getting from businessmen.

People are changing. The young, especially, have different aspirations from the older generation – the – so-called generation gap – and are looking for different things out of life; they have different attitudes towards work and employment and towards employer-employee relations. The situation of older people is changing and not always for the better, the social problems created middle career malaise as reflected in executive obsolescence, redundancy, and forced early retirement and feeling of personal insecurity are becoming more acute. It is no longer true, if it ever was that if an executive is out of work, it is his own fault. Yet the stigma still attaches to such people as is to be seen in the difficulties of re-employment, the absence of proper executive re-training schemes within companies as a means of avoiding redundancy, and the absence of humane properly phased, programmed retirement policies". (Marketing Concepts and Strategies in the Next Decade, edited by Leslie W. Rodger Pg. 30)

2.3 Political/Legal Environment of Business

There is a close relationship between the social environment and the political and legal environment of business. This is because laws are ordinarily passed as a result of social problems and pressures. These laws are allowed to continue to exist even after the need for them had long disappeared. Most of our tax laws are good examples. Let us examine each of political and legal environments more critically.

2.3.1 The Political Environment

Political environments depicted by the attitudes and actions of political and government leaders and legislators do change with ebb and flow of social demands and beliefs. Weihrich and Koontz report that government affects virtually every enterprise and every aspect of life. With respect to business, it acts in two main roles: it promotes and constrains business e.g. it promotes business by stimulating economic expansion and development by providing assistance to small and medium businesses by subsidizing selected industries, by giving tax advantages in certain situations, by supporting research and development and by protecting some businesses through special tariffs. Government is also the biggest customer purchasing goods and services.

2.3.2 The Legal Environment

Government has the important role of constraining and regulating business. Every business is encircled by a web of laws, regulations and court decisions, some of which are designed to protect workers, consumers and communities while others are designed to regulate the behaviors of business owners, managers and their subordinates. Many of these laws are necessary even though some of them become obsolete. Although it is not an easy matter, businessmen and women must foresee and respond to laws that might be passed which may have negative effect on the conduct of business and making some businesses to lose their competitive advantage.

2.4   The Technological Environment

"One of the most pervasive factors in the environment is technology. It is science that provides knowledge, and it is technology that uses it. The term technology refers to the sum total of the knowledge we have of ways to do things. It includes inventions, it includes techniques, and it includes the vast store of organized knowledge about everything from aerodynamics to zoology. But its main influence is on ways of doing things, on how we design, produce, distribute and sell goods as well as services" (Weihrich and Koontz).

2.4.1   The Benefit of Technology

The impact is now felt in government, homes and business e.g. new products are introduced into the market daily. This gives rise to new machines, new tools, raw materials and new services. All these translate to higher output, better standard of living, increased leisure time, etc. the impact of technology can also be viewed from the variety of brands and sizes of different products, e.g. cars, computers, electronic products, aircrafts, ammunitions, etc. now available.

2.4.2   The Problems of Technology

As pervasive and beneficial as technology appears to be, there are problems which every business owner and manager must be aware of and take steps to overcome in order to achieve the purpose and objective of establishing their business. Some of the problems include traffic jams, water and air pollution, energy shortages, loss of privacy (through the application of computer technology), etc.#

2.5.   The Competitive Environment of Business

Competition is another limiting factor to business. To stay in business, there is need to continuously watch the activities of other companies doing the same or similar business.

This has the effect of improving the quality and variety of products and services offering. Competition can take many forms but the most pervasive form of competition is related to price. Because of the high level of poverty in this country, price has become a major determinant in the purchase/spending decision-making process. This is so because the average Nigerian would like to maximize his/her consumption with the meagre income at his/her disposal. This development has seriously affected the quality of products in the Nigerian market. Since "there is no morality in business", most manufacturers and traders have decided to catch in on this lost value from the consumer angle to produce low quality goods for sale at a price that consumers can afford, thereby making abnormal profit. Some of these businesses however, do not last as they may not be able to foresee and respond to changes in tastes and preferences of consumers. The businesses that are able to maintain quality at all times and be satisfied with normal or little profit are likely to last longer. This is because consumers will eventually revert to quality either when income changes or when they have information about the exploitative activities of producers or businessmen who have placed greater emphasis on price rather than satisfaction of consumer wants.

Chapter Three

The Role of Government in Business

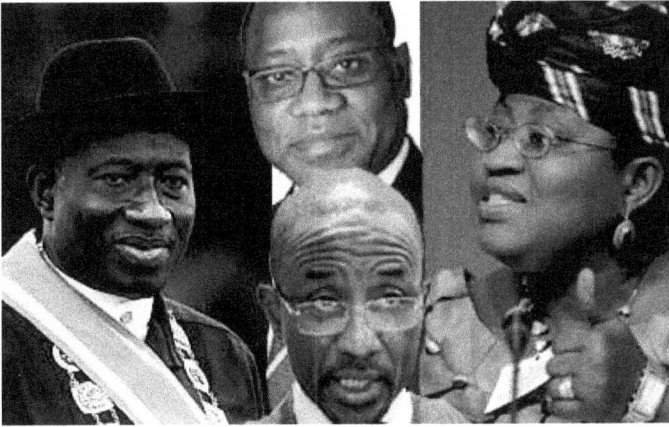

3.0   Government and Business

Governments all over the world play different roles in business. The role played depends on a number of factors. These include the type of economic system in practice e.g. free market mixed or command economy; the type of government or political system e.g. military, democracy, autocracy; the sensitivity or otherwise of the people in government; the level of development of infrastructural facilities; the amount of influence or level of control the government has over natural resources; the interest the government has in participating in business; the level of a country's economic development, etc. A free market economy is one in which business is left in the hands of private sector operators; in a mixed economy, business can be done jointly or severally by both public and private sector operators, while only government is responsible for businesses done in a command economy. Further discussions on this topic will center on the following:

(a) **Regulation and Protection**

(b) **Provision of Infrastructural Facilities**

(c) **Provision of Enabling Environment**

(d) **Supervision and Control**

(e) **Funding, Subsidy and Incentives**

(f) **Setting of Standards.**

3.1   Regulation and Protection

The conduct and practice of business in any society must be regulated and necessary protection provided for those who operate according to the rules. Although businesses form associations to regulate relationships among members and protect the interest of members, it is the responsibility of the government to set standard parameters within which businesses and associations must operate. Government must not only enact legislation, it must also review such legislations to ensure that they are current and potent enough to bring about the desired effects or changes in the business environment. For instance, most governments enact legislation to break certain monopolies in order to engender competition and ensure that consumers are not unnecessarily exploited. Another example is the issue of legislation to control the retail prices of commodities. Sometimes, legislation is put in place to discourage profiteering, hoarding and such other sharp practices.

On the issue of protection, it may be a deliberate policy of government to protect local infant businesses to make them grow to such a size as will enable them to compete with international companies and products. Protection of local businesses is also a way through which government attempts to attain sufficiency in production.

3.2   Provision of Infrastructural Facilities

Businesses require a platform upon which to commence operation otherwise the cost of setting up and ultimately operating the business will be prohibitive. For example, the following are prerequisites to operating a successful business not only in Nigeria but in any other country: availability of good roads, good transportation system, availability of stable energy supply, efficient communication system, availability of a suitable financial system, adequate protection of life and property, guarantee of fundamental human rights, etc.

3.2.1 Availability of Good Roads

The importance of good roads to business cannot be over-emphasized. Roads are required to move raw materials and finished goods to and from the factory to the market(s); they are required to move workers to and from the factory, even production equipment and other facilities need to be moved from one place to another. Road construction requires proper planning and huge capital outlay. If businesses are to embark on this, it may become too expensive to establish some businesses coupled with the fact that the gestation period for such businesses will be unnecessarily prolonged; the cost of the products which are the output of such businesses may be too high for the consumers to afford; if every business has to plan and construct its own road networks, the haphazard nature of the country's road system can only be imagined! It is for these reasons that government must m ake available good network of roads to assist businesses.

3.2.2 Provision of Good Transportation System

Apart from good roads, efficient transportation system is required to facilitate the movement of equipment, raw materials, finished goods and people. Even though businesses will still provide their own transportation fleet, the support of the government is required to enable businesses enjoy economy of scale.

For instance, it is difficult for individual business organisations to embark on rail, air, water and road transport networks because of cost. Movement can be cheaper and faster from the hinterland through the use of specialized transport facilities. Since government controls natural resources in this country, the efficient supply of fuel and gas through pipelines is also better handled by it.

3.2.3   Stable Power Supply

Most businesses require constant and stable power supply to enable them operates effectively and efficiently. The cost of providing this essential service is huge. It is therefore not advisable for individual business organisations to provide them for reasons already stated in the above points. Only businesses that engage in mass production have been able to succeed fairly in establishing and operating their own power supply systems. It would have been better if public supply of power/energy for industrial use were made efficient and stable.

3.2.4 Efficient Communication System

Communication is essential for the success of business. It is also a very expensive facility that individual firms cannot afford. Haphazardness will also be experienced if this service is proliferated. For these reasons, the government has a responsibility for its provision. For instance, it costs millions of dollars to launch a satellite gateway station into the orbit for the purpose of providing telephone, fax and internet services. The equipment for establishing telephone exchanges and radio/telephone stations/channels as well as radio-phone services is equally exorbitant and prohibitive for individual business organisations.

3.2.5 Suitable and Efficient Financial System

Businesses need agents to keep and transfer funds for them as well as offer financial support where necessary. It is the responsibility of government to ensure that banks, insurance companies, bureau de change, etc. are established to provide the needed support for business organisations and entrepreneurs. All these must be established in their different categories. For instance, in the banking sector, there must be development banks to provide long-term funds, merchant banks to provide wholesale and medium-term funds and commercial banks to provide short-term funds, keep deposits, make transfers and provide other funds, and checking accounts for businesses. Insurance companies must be available to insure businesses against unforeseen losses and perils, etc.

3.2.6 Adequate Protection of Life and Property

The environment in which business is done must be safe not only for the life of the business owner and his staff, but also for his/her equipment and goods. Protection from the police and other law enforcement agencies against armed robbery attacks, illegal conversion of assets, etc, is a necessary prerequisite in any business environment. Where businessmen/women, employees, suppliers and other stakeholders in a business are killed or maimed without justice being done and the wares of the business organisations are stolen without recourse to the law enforcement agents to help out with recovery and justice, investment will be highly discouraged.

3.2.7 Guaranteed Fundamental Human Rights

This has to do with freedom of movement, freedom of speech, freedom of association, freedom of worship, etc, of the owners of the business and their employees as well as other stakeholders. Where freedom in all these areas is not guaranteed, potential businesses will definitely not come on board. For instance, a businessman or woman is likely to immediately close up his business if he/she is discriminated against, in terms of race, tribe, color, religion, etc., and move to a more investment friendly environment.

3.3 Provision of Enabling Environment

All the factors already discussed above are relevant here. The point to emphasize here is that where the government is not in position or is practically unable to provide these facilities, it should do everything possible to encourage their provision through other means e.g. through privatization, private sector initiative, foreign direct investment, etc. An example is what is presently happening to the communication, power supply and some other sectors of the Nigeria economy.

3.4 Supervision and Control of Business

It is part of the responsibility of the government to supervise and control the conduct of business in the country. One objective of this is to reduce sharp practices to the barest minimum, if it cannot be totally eliminated. Some good examples of sectors of the Nigerian economy that are closely supervised and controlled are banking, insurance, food and drugs, education as well as petroleum, power and telecommunications. The Central Bank of Nigeria (CBN_ and the Nigeria Deposit Insurance Corporation (NDIC) are the organs through which the banking sector is supervised and controlled. The Credit Policy Guidelines are issued annually by the CBN, Bankers' Tariffs are approved and reviewed as and when necessary while advertisements by banks must first be approved by the CBN before they are published. Various banking examinations and audits are also conducted by the CBN and NDIC apart from the fact that banks render regular returns of their activities to these bodies. The Federal Ministry of Health controls the food and drugs sectors. This is achieved through the National Food and Drugs Administration and Control (NAFDAC). We have all heard about the destruction of millions of naira worth of unfit food and drugs imported into this country at different times. The education sector is supervised at the local, state and federal levels. There is no doubt that the raging controversy about external degree programs and NECO versus WAEC has seen the sector coming out better. For the petroleum sector, we are witnesses to developments aimed at making the sector meet the needs, yearnings and aspirations of the citizenry. The NDDC bill was recently passed by the National Assembly to help in the development of the oil producing communities. What is happening in both the power and telecommunications sectors are also of special interest if both sectors are to catch up with world development. The National Communications Commission (NCC) is responsible for the supervision of the telecommunications sector through the issue of licenses, etc. the insurance sector is going through tremendous changes under the supervision of the National Insurance Commission (NAICOM). The Commission receives regular returns from all insurance companies. It also conducts audits and investigations on them from time to time. The National Broadcasting Commission (NBC) is responsible for the supervision and control of the radio and television broadcasting sectors of the Nigerian economy.

3.5   Funding, Subsidy and Incentives

Government has the responsibility of providing the enabling environment for ensuring that businesses are properly funded. It also should provide subsidy and incentives to deserving businesses. In the agricultural sector, the Agricultural Credit Guarantee Scheme (ACGS) and the Nigerian Agricultural and Rural Development Bank are two efforts of the Federal Government at ensuring that farmers have access to funds. National Economic Reconstruction Fund (NERFUND), Nigeria Industrial Development Bank (NIDB) and Nigeria Bank for Commerce and Industry (NBCI) – both now combined and re-christened Bank of Industry (BOI) are efforts geared towards ensuring that industrialists have access to funds. The efforts of Nigeria Export-Import Bank (NEXIM) with its Export Stimulation Load (ESL), Refinancing and Rediscounting Facility (RRF), etc. are efforts aimed at encouraging exports. There are a host of other incentives for exporters while the Nigerian Export Promotion Commission (NEPC) is continuing in its struggle to make life better for exporters. Subsidy is not a common occurrence in Nigeria. However, government should look into this area of encouraging small and medium scale businesses under the poverty alleviation scheme of the Federal and State Governments.

3.6   Setting of Standards

Since it is the responsibility of the government to protect its citizens against unfair trade practices, it should set, maintain and control the quality of products that are produced and offered for sale by manufacturers. In Nigeria, this task is achieved through the Standards Organisation of Nigeria (SON). Manufacturers are expected to comply with the standards established by SON for their various products. In some cases, SON works in conjunction with NAFDAC, especially on food and drug products.

Chapter Four

Running a Successful Business

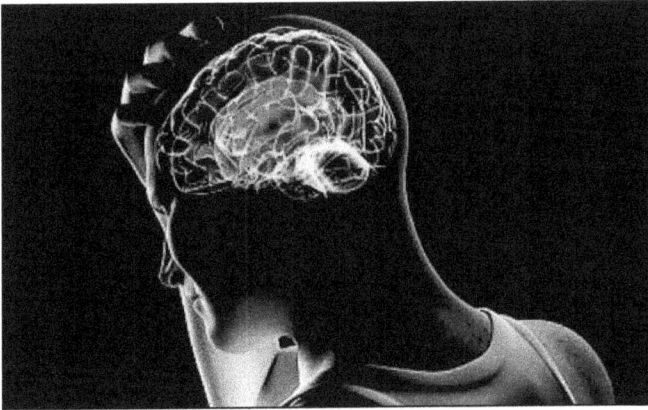

4.0   Business Failure: An Avoidable Headache

Business failure is a regular and recurring problem. It is a matter for concern to business analysts and consultants. Failure in business is avoidable if necessary precautions are taken to play according to the rules instead of playing to the gallery. Starting and running a successful business is a serious matter and must be given due consideration and attention it deserves. The fact that a business succeeds today is not a guarantee that it will be on ground tomorrow. Circumstances keep changing: it could be favorable, unfavorable, harsh, hostile, depressed, predictable, unpredictable, etc. There are times when the situation is so favorable that even a fool could make it in business. Such situations are very rare. Therefore, business should not be left to chance, as it is not a game of chance. Neither should it be left entirely to luck but to a strong determination to succeed.

Experience has shown that running a successful business could be as easy as ABC, if necessary precautions are not neglected and certain rules are observed.

4.1   Key Success Factors

Factors that determine the success or otherwise of a business can be grouped under two main headings – internal and external.

4.1.1   Internal Factors

These are factors well known by or with which owners and managers of the business are familiar. In most cases, these factors are controllable. Some of these factors include: Capital, Capability, Collateral, Qualifications, Character, Continuity, Record Keeping, Insurance and Overtrading.

4.1.1.1 Capital

This is a very important aspect of business. There is virtually no business that can be done without capital. Lack of or insufficient capital is one factor that kills business fast. A businessman or woman must give due consideration to the nature, type and amount of capital required for the business to commence operation and at all times when changes are to be made to the nature, type and size of business or product or when a diversification is contemplated. Business operators in Nigeria do not consider feasibility study as important. They also do not know the value of consultants. When some of them employ consultants, they may not pay their dues/fees or they pay an amount not commensurate with the services rendered and not in line with the agreement earlier reached.

If a proper feasibility study has been conducted, it would have indicated the total amount of capital required broken down into amount to be committed to fixed assets acquisition, working capital and contingencies. It would also have indicated the time when funds are required for each of these categories of capital and suggesting sources of raising additional capital required to complement the amount available to the proprietor or promoter of the business.

The raising of sufficient capital requires proper planning and foresight. It should not be a matter of "firefighting" because money is not easy to get. To get it as and when necessary, there is need for forward planning.

4.1.1.2 Capability

Many people engage in business without assessing their capability to do the particular type of business. Even where all the other ingredients for running a successful business are present, the absence or lack of this particular ingredient could cause the failure of an otherwise potentially successful business concern. A person intending to start a business should evaluate himself to determine whether he has all it takes to run a business of the size and magnitude he has in contemplation. The same evaluation process should be adopted when the business is to be expanded or diversified. Some people have serious limitations as to the number of people they can control, the amount of money they can manage, the number of offices, vehicles, product lines, etc. they can oversee at any point in time. Such people will misbehave if they are exposed beyond their limit. This is the reason why some businesses succeed at startup and as they grow they fail fast as growth and expansion overstretches the limit of the owner. It is sometimes more difficult to sustain a business than to start it up.

Important factors to consider under this heading include: ability to employ the right men, machines, materials and methods; ability to take the right decisions at the right time;

ability to foresee and forecast the future to a reasonable extent; ability to plan and operate the plan; ability to determine the company's mission, vision, goals and objectives; ability to adapt to changing circumstances knowing fully well that "no condition is permanent"; ability to manage resources effectively and efficiently, ability to analyses situations critically and take the best option, etc.

The adage "do not bite more than you can chew" is very relevant here. If a person fails to evaluate his capability before going into business, the result will be failure. Therefore, it is better to "think before you do" as the consequences of doing otherwise might be disastrous.

4.1.1.3 Collateral

This has to do with tangible assets, which can be pledged or relied upon by creditors when the business decides to obtain credit. When a business is not able to obtain fund as and when it is required because of lack of collateral, it could mean the end of that business. During the good days of a business, it should strive to develop collateral that could be used as a cushion when things reverse.

4.1.1.4 Qualifications

It is important to note that adequate qualifications are required for certain types of business. Emphasis here may not actually be on paper qualification but on adequate training and some useful experience on the type of business venture chosen as well as the technical competence. This helps to build confidence on the part of the business person to deal decisively with issues and problems to the satisfaction of customers. Where the business person has to refer to someone else before responding to problems, customers usually have a feeling of incompetence and patronage may cease there and then. This is the beginning of failure as such information spread like wild fire. Closely related to the issue of qualification is deep knowledge of the type of business chosen and understanding of the tricks played by customers and employees. Ability to read and write and issue written documents to customers is part of the deal. Some businesses are not able to exploit opportunities open to them because of lack of ability to read and write. A minimum level of education is important for any type of business nowadays. Customers prefer to deal with well-trained, qualified, articulate and literate business persons rather than stack illiterates.

4.1.1.5 Character

This has to do with the personal qualities of the business person. Some of the personal qualities required to operate a successful business include objectivity, fairness, stamina, ingenuity, enthusiasm, optimism, courage, creativity, endurance, judgment, resourcefulness and leadership ability. The person(s) behind a business must assess himself/themselves on a regular basis to determine whether the demands of the business can be met at all times. What is the benefit of setting up a business if one is not able to give what it takes to make it succeed? For example, withdrawing or relenting in the midst of a crisis instead of being optimistic and enthusiastic that the problem will soon roll away may mark the end of an otherwise potentially successful business. Honesty, they say, is the best policy. Therefore, honesty and integrity must be part of the guiding principles of business if it is to succeed. Where distrust sets into the relationship between a business and its customers, staff and other stakeholders, the life of the business may be brought to an abrupt and premature end. The character of the business owner determines his/her attitude to nurture the business to an enviable standard. The result of a negative attitude will spell doom for the business. Character will also shape the relationship between the business and all stakeholders. A good character is like a soothing balm while bad relationship kills business.

4.1.1.6 Continuity

Most businesses are centered on a single individual i.e. the owner or proprietor. The health condition of that owner determines the degree of consistency and the regularly with which business is done. This may affect patronage, thus making the business epileptic. This epileptic condition may persist for as long as the proprietor lives but upon his death, the business comes to a final stop. Since the owner has not reposed confidence in anybody to manage the business for him the venture dies upon the demise of the owner.

This is why wise business people employ managers or train a child to take over from them and they delegate a high level of authority and responsibility to them while they are still alive as a way of training them. This is the strategy adopted by Oba Oladele Olashore for the running of Lead Merchant Bank; Otunba Subomi Balogun has one of his son as the Managing Director of City Securities Limited, Henry Fajemirokun's son has successfully been managing Henry Stevens, since the demise of his father; some of Late Bashorun MKO Abiola's businesses are now doing well in the hands of competent managers even after his departure from the face of mother earth while others have become moribund due to family squabbles.

Death is certain to occur and those businessmen who think the secret of their business belongs to them only are indirectly affecting the continuity of the business after their death. In view of this fact, even if all the people cannot be trusted, there are still some who could be trusted without regretting it. A business proprietor has the onerous task of identifying such people who could take over from them and help ensure the continuity of the business.

4.1.1.7 Record Keeping

Many business people do not believe in keeping the records of their transactions and thus they are not able to monitor progress and performance. Some even believe that they will pay high tax to the government if they keep records. This is complete ignorance and there is need to change this type of orientation. Every business should keep accurate records of operations. This will provide information for control (i.e. for monitoring performance to determine whether set goals are being achieved or not) and for further planning. Records should be kept for every aspect of the company's operation e.g. personnel, administration, production, sales, costs, inventory, profit/loss, banking transactions, sources and uses of funds, etc. A business should also obtain and keep records concerning the activities of competitors. In these days of back duty audits conducted on companies by the governments, it is important to keep accurate records of operations and financial transactions. Apart from the proprietor and government, records must be kept to satisfy all other stakeholders e.g. shareholders and investors in limited liability companies. By keeping adequate and accurate records bias and distrust is removed from the mind of these stakeholders.

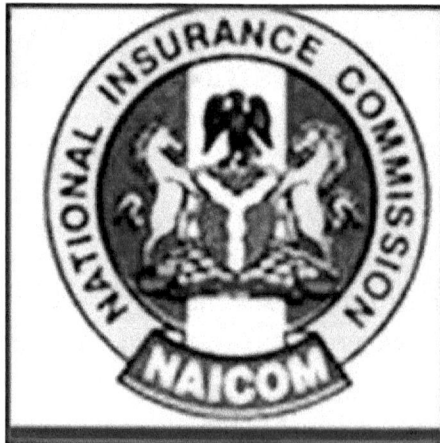

4.1.1.8 Insurance

The purpose of insurance is to help businessmen mitigate their losses in case of the occurrence of any peril. However, most businessmen are ignorant of this fact. Those of them that know about insurance are not willing to pay premium as they feel this will constitute a strain on their finances. Some also do not believe in the concept of insurance while some others have the extreme believe that all will be well, at all times. These set of people have forgotten that when the sinner suffers, the righteous partake in the suffering and that the whole world is full of good and evil. Because of pervasiveness of uncertainties in the business environment, it is important to seek information on and take up such insurances as would be appropriate to keep the business going when unforeseen and unexpected contingencies present themselves.

4.1.1.9 Overtrading

This is a condition in which the capital and funds of a business venture are overstretched thereby creating a long span of illiquidity and eventual insolvency. The pressure that is brought to bear on the business becomes unbearable and ultimately there is a run on the business leading to a total collapse. Business owners should avoid overtrading, as it is one of the potent pills that aid the premature death of businesses. It is better to develop gradually and grow consistently over time, rather than grow big within shortest time and burst. The growth of an enterprise should be planned and managed. Even where thousands of suppliers are willing to grant credit, the business must evaluate each source of credit, to determine which ones are suitable and convenient. If all forms of credit options open to the enterprise are taken without due consideration, it may turn to be a trap or snare to kill the business of an unsuspecting proprietor.

4.1.1.10   Separation of Personal and Business Funds

Inability of business owners to separate personal funds from business funds usually creates an illusion and ultimately results in overspending of the business funds. This phenomenon has led to the demise of a large number of business concerns. People who intend to succeed in business must imbibe the discipline of separation of personal from business funds.

4.1.2   External Factors

These factors are external to the organisation and are largely beyond the control of the business owner or his managers. We will consider these factors under the following headings: Public supply of utilities, government policy, religion, natural disasters, innovation, competition, inflation and market preferences.

4.1.2.1 Public Supply of Utilities

Where a business relies solely on utilities supplied by public enterprise, as is the case in Nigeria (e.g. power supply), the non-availability and irregular supply of these utilities might put the business in a comatose situation. This is true especially where there are no alternatives or where alternatives are very expensive and require long time to install. It is therefore important for a business proprietor to analyse the situation and make necessary arrangement for alternative supply of these utilities before commencing operation. Where such arrangement is not made, it may disrupt operations or make the company to grind to a halt.

4.1.2.2 Government Policy

Government policy has a lot of influence on business and thus deserves to be given due consideration at all times. Where government policy is consistent, business may be able to predict the direction of policy and therefore take necessary proactive steps to mitigate effect(s) of expected policy on operations. From experience, government policy in Nigeria has so far been largely inconsistent and unstable. There have been as many changes in policy as the number of people who have led us as Presidents or Ministers and Governors at the different levels of governance. The sporadic changes we had witnessed in government policy had had tremendous negative effect on business in some sectors of the economy. A few examples will confirm this. Before the ban on the use of phones for commercial business, it had been the mainstay of many business centers in the country. Government had to put a peg on this business in just one day because of a few people who were doing the business illegally or in a dubious manner and government was not able to police them properly. Several government policies have impacted negatively on the banking sector because of their inconsistency e.g. interest rate policy, exchange rate policy, credit allocation and loan policies, capital, licenses, etc.

The negative effect of some of these policies actually contributed to the collapse of a large number of the failed banks. The policy on excise duty, customs tariff, export and import documentation and inspection requirements, etc. have also affected the lives of many companies in the production sector of the Nigerian economy. There was a lot of confusion in 2000/2001 on policy of education with particular reference to the establishment of satellite campuses of universities. People needed education and the main campuses of universities were not in position to admit up to 10% of these desirous students. As at now many deserving students are still not able to gain admission to universities even as the number of universities has more than doubled.

A virile way to create a balance is to establish outreach centers or satellite campuses for courses requiring no practicals. The responsibility of the government in this case is to state conditions for establishing these satellite/outreach centers to enable them meet or maintain minimum standards, instead of proscribing them.

4.1.2.3 Religion

Depending on the nature of business, religion could be an important determinant of the success or failure of some business ventures. For instance, Sharia is already taking its toll on alcohol business in some of the Northern States of Nigeria. Rearing and selling of pork and pork products is also dangerous in these Sharia States, as well as selling packaged/tinned food items containing beef without proper

Church and Mosques in Abuja FCT

education to convince Muslims that the items do no contain pork meat. In all these locations, there must be some craze for Arabic attires, especially for women and people who are fast enough to establish business in this area will no doubt succeed. The adoption of a state religion may or may not bring the life of some businesses to an abrupt and unplanned end, depending on the number of adherents of the state religion.

4.1.2.4 Natural Disasters

Natural and other disasters like flood, earthquake, landslide, thunder storm, fire, drought, excessive rain, inclement weather, etc. usually have deleterious effects on business, when they occur. Most of these disasters occur in a mysterious manner and the occurrence of any one of them may make a business to close shop, not only temporarily, but also permanently.

4.1.2.5 Innovation

Innovation has both positive and negative effects on business. When innovation is frequent, it may send the less innovative ventures out of business, while the innovative one records great success. The success may be initially expensive but becomes cheaper as the number of companies competing with the innovator reduces and the innovator eventually becomes a monopolist. The lesson to be learnt is that wherever one intends to venture into a high innovative and volatile business, coping strategies must be developed to avoid rushing in and out.

4.1.2.6 Competition

Nobody goes into business without considering how well others already in the business are doing and the fact that other people with the same idea will come in the business later. Competition is good as it brings about improvement in the quality of goods and services as well as in the way things are done. Competition, where it leads to mass production, also brings about reduction in prices of goods and services. On the other hand, competition couldn't be distinctive e.g. where an already established big business with all its might is in competition with small businesses. Sometimes, also, price competition may be adopted by some businesses to consider the nature of competition and the effect it will have on his proposed business before going headlong into the business.

4.1.2.7 Inflation

This is a cankerworm that besets plans, especially in terms of finance. Where a business had planned to spend 10million naira to purchase certain items and there is a 40% rise in the level of inflation, about 14million will now be spent to purchase the items. This will seriously affect the profit as it is not possible to transfer all costs to the customers in all circumstances. To succeed in an inflationary economy, a business owner must put strategies in place to hedge against inflation or at least mitigate its effect on operations.

4.1.2.8 Market Preferences

Consumer tastes and preferences change from time to time. This is the reason a product in vogue today loses its pride of place tomorrow. Sometimes the change in preferences may not be in terms of the quality of the product, rather it may be related to delivery, packaging, size, usage, etc. A business that is not able to adapt to these changes will fail. Therefore, business proprietors should regularly research into current potential change in the preferences of its customers in order to serve them better.

Chapter Five

FORMS OF OWNERSHIP OF BUSINESS

5.0   Forms of Ownership

Ownership of business can be in three main forms irrespective of the nature of business, whether we are talking of manufacturing, distribution or services. The three main forms of ownership are:

1.   Single Owner:

These are businesses owned by only one person. They are usually referred to as sole proprietorships or sole traders.

2.   Multiple Ownerships:

Owners could be by many individuals, individuals and corporate organisations, individuals and government(s) as well as corporate bodies and governments or a combination of these. The forms of business organisations here include: (a) Partnerships (b) Private Limited Liability Companies (c) Public Limited Liability Companies, (d) Co-operative Societies, (e) International Companies, (f) Multi-national Corporations and (g) Non-Governmental Organisations (NGOs), etc.

3.   Government Ownership:

These are companies owned solely by the government e.g. public corporations, government companies and parastatals.

Please note that sole proprietorships and partnerships are usually referred to as firms; other forms of business with multiple owners are called companies while government companies are commonly known as public corporations. The category of business in which you find most people in Nigeria is sole proprietorship. The rest of this chapter discusses in detail the different forms of business organisations.

5.1   Sole Proprietorship Business

This is a type of business that is owned and managed by only one person. It is from this concept that the name "sole proprietorship" was derived. The following are the other characteristics of the sole proprietorship business.

5.1.1   Full Personal Control

Owning and running one's own business makes one to be independent. The sole proprietor is free to decide what he wants to do and when to do it. He decides what to produce or sell, where to locate the business based on his personal preferences and financial commitment to the business, when to open and close, when to diversify or change his line of business, etc. All the profits accruing from the business belongs to him and he makes quick decisions since he does not need to consult with anybody, especially when there is an emergency. This could enhance his profit and attract greater patronage to him. For instance, if he receives reliable information that price of the item he sells is likely to rise from the source in two weeks' time; he could raise money quickly and purchase large quantity of the item before the price rise. The difference between the old and the new price is likely to be additional profit. This personal control of the business brings him into close contact with his customers and employees. This has the effect of increasing productivity and helping to solve problems faster. If customers' and employees' problems are solved quickly, they become more loyal to the organisation.

5.1.2 Simple to Organize

The sole proprietorship business is the simplest form of business organisation in view of its ease of entry and exit as well as the absolute absence of government control on this form of business. There is no formality involved in setting up a sole proprietorship business. A man could decide to buy and resell anything at any time without necessarily having to register a business name. The sole proprietor pays tax as an individual and not on his profit. So, he is not required by the tax authority to submit an account before paying tax or before obtaining a tax clearance certificate.

5.1.3 Small Size

The size of the business is limited to the amount of capital at the disposal of the proprietor. Usually, this is made up of his personal savings or borrowings from friends and relatives. Even where the sole proprietor decides to borrow from banks, he will need to provide acceptable collateral security, which is usually not available. The reason for this heavy demand for collateral is that banks and other financial institutions are reluctant to entrust their funds to the control of one man whose activities they may not have control over. This limits the ability of the sole proprietor to expand his business. Size also limits the ability of the proprietor to recruit experts to assist him to run the business.

5.1.4 Lack of Continuity

A sole proprietorship business depends and relies largely on its owner. Such a business will come to an abrupt end when the owner dies or becomes seriously ill. When this happens, the staff members of the sole proprietor all lose their jobs and there is no assurance that suppliers and creditors will be able to get paid for goods supplied and services rendered.

5.1.5   Unlimited Liability

The liabilities of the owner of a sole proprietorship business are not limited to the amount of capital contributed by him, as is the case with incorporated companies. A sole proprietor could lose all he has in the event of failure of his business until he is able to meet all the financial obligations of the business. In the event of failure of his business, a sole proprietor may have to face bankruptcy proceedings in the court if he is unable to meet the obligations of the business even after selling some of his personal belongings.

5.1.6   No Separate Legal Entity

The owner of a sole proprietorship business and his business are one and the same. The law does not confer a separate legal personality (entity) on sole proprietorship business. Therefore, when a sole proprietorship business is sued, it is the owner that is sued. The converse is true.

5.1. A Advantages of Sole Proprietorship

The sole proprietorship business possesses a number of advantages over other forms of business organisations. They provide most of the personal and loyal services like shoe shining, barbing, sewing, painting, welding, watch repairing, carpet/rug cleaning, shoe making and repairing, radio/television repairing, etc. The advantages are the reasons this type of business is in large number and include the following:

5.1.A1 Ease of Entry

No special formalities and no formal qualifications are required to start a sole proprietorship business. Except for professions where licenses and or registration are required (e.g. accountancy, engineering, medicine and law). Business is open to anyone in other professions/occupations. For instance, nothing stops an accountant from setting up a block-making business or to engage in the selling of building materials.

5.1.A2 Adaptability/Dynamism

We are in a changing environment. Large businesses choose their business lines and changing the business line is often a difficult decision to take. A sole proprietorship business can easily adapt and/or change line of business, method of operation, staff, etc. For instance, I can sell cars this month, change to foodstuffs next month and move to book selling later, depending on changing circumstances and environmental conditions.

5.1.A3 The Sole Proprietorship Business Pays No Tax

Only the owner of a sole proprietorship pays tax. The business pays no tax as the law recognizes the business and its owner to be the same person – the owner cannot be separated from the business neither can the business be separated from the owner.

5.1.A4 Independence

The sole proprietor has the latitude to choose what to do, how to do it and when to do it. He is his own master and derives high level of satisfaction form running his own business. For instance, the sole proprietor can choose his time of operation and this can change from day to day or from week to week depending on the nature of business at hand. He can choose to sleep in the morning and work at night. This is not usually the case with large business. Organisations. A pure water manufacturer, for example, can choose to produce all night and distribute wares during the day.

5.1. A5   Low Running Costs

Sole proprietorship businesses are known to be less expensive to operate. For instance, a man could convert his outer sitting room into a shop. By so doing, he will not pay rent on premises. He can also enlist services of his wife and children, thereby not paying any wages or salaries to employed staff. Sometimes, low running costs result in higher profits and gradual growth and longtime survival of sole proprietorship businesses.

5.1.A6 Personal Touch/Close Relationship

There is personal touch in the sole proprietorship business. It is this personal touch that makes some customers and suppliers to deal with the business or to want to continue to deal with the business. The close relationship and personal rapport between the owner and his employees also helps the business immensely. In some of the big organisations, some of the employees and customers do not have the opportunity of a close relationship with the Managing Director.

5.1.A7 Low Capital

Sole Proprietorship businesses do not require large amounts of capital to start or operate. A mechanic could set up a workshop with as low as N10, 000 and a barber with less; a shop owner could commence business with as low as N5, 000. Even with this low capital, a shop owner could carry a large variety of commodities.

5.1. A8   Quick Decision Making

In view of the fact that management and control are concentrated in one person, decision-making becomes fast and as experience grows, it becomes a routine. This leads to dexterity and greater efficiency, thus making the sole proprietor to become an expert in his chosen field. This is true only for those who stay long in their lines of business before changing. For those who change their lines of business often, it is a case of "a rolling stone gathers no moss".

5.1.A9 Avoidance of Wastes

As a result of the absolute lack of bureaucracy in the operation of a sole proprietorship business, wastage in time, effort, money, materials, etc. can be avoided, or minimized if at all they occur. This explains why the efficiency rate of personal businesses is higher than those of multiple owners.

5.1. A10   Providing Service for Big Business

Large business organisations necessarily require the services of small firms in a number of areas, especially in areas where it will not be cost effective to provide these services in-house e.g. most oil companies hire the services of transporters to move their products and staff. By so doing, the cost of maintaining a fleet of vehicles, paying salaries and allowances to drivers, mechanics and allied staff, arranging person, etc. for them, and various other costs are avoided. Sole proprietorship businesses are therefore better able to handle outsourcing more efficiently.

5.1.B   Disadvantages of Sole Proprietorship

Despite the numerous advantages of the sole proprietorship form of business, it has some disadvantages. These are discussed below.

5.1. B1 High Failure Rate

The relative ease of starting a sole proprietorship business encourages all kinds of people to jump into it. Some are highly optimistic; some completely planless, unfocussed, and disillusioned, while a host of others do not have a faint idea of the type of business they intend to start. They are just infatuated by the success and prosperity of people already doing that particular type of business. Apart from the optimistic and focused set of people, a host of the others are likely to fail. This explains the high failure rate of the sole proprietorship business all over the world. Also, the ill-health, accident or death of the proprietor, most of the time, bring the business to an abrupt end, if he has no suitable successor.

5.1.B2 Shortage of Capital for Expansion

Every businessman or woman desires growth. This cannot often be achieved through one's own resources and personal savings. Also, there is a limit to the amount an individual can borrow from banks and other financial institutions, even from friends and relatives. This shortage of financial resources results in financial handicaps and affects the ability of the sole proprietorship business to grow and expand to the level desired by the owner. It also weakens the firm's ability to compete in the market, especially where others are using improved methods of operation that help to reduce costs and it has no money to follow suit.

5.1.B3 Lack of Specializations/Division of Labor

The owner of a sole proprietorship business is a generalist – a manager, director, storekeeper, accountant/book-keeper, chief buyer, salesman, chief security officer, etc. This suggests low degree or lack of specialization and division of labor. The proprietor wants to be everywhere at the same time and this is not possible. The effect is that because everything about the business is concentrated in only one person, new ideas are usually difficult to come by except those of the sole proprietor himself.

5.1. B4Difficulty of Separation of Self from the Business

One major disadvantage of the sole proprietorship business is that it is difficult to separate the business from the owner. Anything that happens to the business will affect the owner and vice versa. If the owner is sued in a law court for instance, it will affect his nosiness, as he will not be able to carry out his enterprise for as long as the suit lasts. This is because the business has no separate legal entity. In the same way, there is no separation between the assets of the business and the owner of the business. The sole proprietor is fully responsible for all the loans and debts contracted by the business and his personal belongings could be sold to defray these debts.

5.2   The Partnership Form of Business

The partnership business is an extension of the sole proprietorship business. This type of business organisation is usually formed with a view to overcoming some of the disadvantages of the sole proprietorship business. This assertion will come to light as we discuss the features and reasons for forming partnership businesses.

5.2.1   Characteristics of Partnership Business

Partnership is the relationship, which subsists between persons carrying on business in common with a view to make profit. The following are the major characteristics of this form of business.

5.2.1.1 Ownership and Control

The number of members in a partnership business (i.e. owners) is between two (2) and twenty (20) persons. This definitely holds better prospect for a partnership business, as many people are involved in the management and control of the business. Specializations and division of labor also set in. The owners of a partnership business are called "members".

5.2.1.2 Size of Business

The size of a business owned by two persons has the potential of being larger than that of a single person. It follows therefore that the size of a business with ownership by twenty persons will definitely be much larger.

5.2.1.3 Capital

More people are involved in a partnership business. As they pool their resources together, the business is able to raise a larger amount of capital. Thus, expansion is easier in a partnership business than in sole proprietorship. It is also easier to raise additional capital in view of the number of persons involved. The worth of twenty persons is definitely likely to be higher than that of a single person. The capital of a partnership business is provided in an agreed ratio.

5.2.1.4 Agreement

An important feature of a partnership business is an agreement between the partners. The agreement provides a working relationship between the partners and covers all areas where misunderstanding may arise between them.

5.2.1.5 Profits and Losses

The profits of a partnership business belong to all the partners and are shared as provided for in the partnership agreement. Losses are also shared in the same proportion.

5.2.1.6 Unlimited Liability

Just as in the case of sole proprietorship business, the liabilities of partners in a partnership business are not limited to the amount of capital they have contributed or have undertaken to contribute. In the event of business failure, all the partners are responsible for the partnership debts up to the limit of their personal possessions.

5.2.1.7 Registration and Formality

No registration or formality is required of a partnership business except in the following cases:

(a) The making of an agreement (this may be unwritten and informal. Where this is the case, the law requires that provisions in the partnership Act/Law will guide the partners' relationship).

(b) If the business is carried on using the names of the owners/members of the partnership (where the partnership is run under a name different from the proper names of the owners, the firm must be registered).

(c) If no member enjoys limited liability (where any of the members intend to enjoy limited liability, such a member becomes a limited partner and registration is required). Limited partnership is discussed later in this chapter.

5.2.1.8 Publication of Accounts and Taxation

A partnership business is not required to publish its accounts for public consumption. The accounts prepared are just for the use of partners for the purpose of determining the profit of the firm and the entitlement of each partner, or if a loss, how to make it good. In the same way as sole proprietorship business, a partnership firm does not pay tax on the business profit(s). rather, each of the partners in the firm pay tax, as individuals, on all their sources of income, including the partnership business.

5.2.1.9   Risk of Dissolution

When the going is good, a partnership business gets on well. However, a simple disagreement or misunderstanding between the partners may bring the life of the firm to an end. Also, the death of a partner automatically operates to dissolve the partnership business in accordance with the partnership law. If other partners decide that the firm should continue, a new partnership agreement becomes necessary which will exclude the dead partner.

5.2.2. Reasons for Forming Partnership

There are many reasons why people form partnership businesses. Some of these reasons are discussed in the following sections.

5.2.2.1 To increase the Capital of a Business

Since up to twenty persons can form a partnership, some sole proprietorship businesses that are interested in increasing their capital base may prefer to invite other people to join their business instead of borrowing from the banks and paying high interests. A partnership business will also be able to borrow more money for business than sole proprietorship, as banks will be more comfortable to lend to a group than to entrust their money in the hands of a single person.

5.2.2.2 For New and Better Ideas

Twenty people could generate better ideas than only one person. This is supported by the adage which says, "two heads are better than one".

5.2.2.3 For Greater Skill and Better Management Ability

Each member of a partnership firm possesses skill, which is different from those of other members. The management ability of each member is also more likely to be different. When different skills and managerial capabilities are combined, the business that evolves from this "pooling of resources" would be better and stronger.

5.2.2.4 For Specializations and Division of Labor.

A partnership allows for partners to exhibit specialization amongst themselves. As a result of this, the entire functions of the partnership can be shared between the partners. This will ensure improvement in the quality of work or services rendered by the partnership business.

5.2.3   Kinds of Partnership

There are only two kinds of partnership, even though there could be different types of partners. A partnership could be either:

(a) Ordinary partnership, or

(b) Limited partnership

5.2.3.1 Ordinary Partnership

This is the most common form of partnership and is the one in which all the partners have equal powers and responsibilities. These powers and responsibilities include taking part in the management of the firm, sharing from the profits and/or losses of the firm and liability for the debts of the partnership business.

5.2.3.2 Limited Partnership

This is a partnership business in which one or more partners have their liabilities limited to the amount of capital invested in the business. The partner(s) with limited liability is/are called "limited partner(s)" and do not take part in the management of the business. In any limited partnership, there must be at least one ordinary partner who is responsible for the day-to-day management of the firm and responsible for all the debts of the firm.

5.4   Types of Partner

The partnership business provides various options to accommodate different types of investors. A partner could be any of the following:

(a) Ordinary/General/Active partner

(b) Limited partner

(c) Nominal partner

(d) Sleeping partner

(e) Silent partner

(f) Principal/Senior partner

(g) Managing partner

(h) Secret partner

5.2.4.1 Ordinary Partner

This is a partner who contributes money and takes part in the running of the day-to-day affairs of the firm. He shares in the profits/losses of the firm and is liable, with the other partners (except for the limited partner(s)) for the debts of the business. He is also called a General or Active Partner.

5.2.4.2 Limited Partner

This partner contributes money for the running of the business but does not take part in the running of the affairs of the firm. His liability is limited to the amount of capital he has contributed or undertaken to contribute to the business.

5.2.4.3 Nominal Partner

This is a partner who allows his name to be used by the firm without playing any active role in the running of the business, sometimes not even contributing any money. This arrangement is made by wealthy, notable or popular persons in the society to assist relations, friends or colleagues in business to attract patronage. People would be inclined to do business with the firm because of the notable/popular person's membership of the firm.

5.2.4.4 Sleeping Partner

A sleeping partner is one who chooses to contribute money for the partnership business but does not take part in management. He is however responsible, like others, for the liability/debts of the firm.

5.2.4.5 Silent Partner

This is a partner who does not take active part in the management of the firm but he is nonetheless known as a partner. He is often referred to as a dormant partner.

5.2.4.6 Principal/Senior Partner

This is a partner with a large amount of capital in the firm. It follows therefore that he also controls management and his decisions and actions carry heavy weight. The other partners will then be referred to as junior partners or sometimes as ordinary partners.

5.2.4.7 Managing Partner

This is the partner assigned the task of effectively managing partnership business. Other partners who take part in the management are only to assist the Managing Partner.

5.2.4.8 Secret Partner

This partner takes active part in the running of the business but he is not known to the public as a partner as his name does not feature in the partners' list.

5.2.4 Disadvantages of Partnership

The partnership business has more or less the same disadvantages with the sole proprietorship business. An additional disadvantages however, is the fact that there could be misunderstanding between the partners. Technically, when a partner pulls away from a partnership business, that marks the end of the firm. Other members could however continue the business under a new agreement and a new name.

5.3 Private and Public Limited Liability Companies

These are otherwise known as incorporated companies. They develop from the need for more capital just as the partnership business developed out of the need for more capital than the sole proprietor could provide. A limited liability company is, in law, regarded as a separate legal entity different from its owners. It is an artificial person, which is able to enter into contracts in its own right, sued and be sued in its own name, just like an ordinary person. However, an incorporated company differs from ordinary person in that it can only act through its properly constituted agents, exercise only those powers and only those functions permitted by its instrument of incorporation (i.e. Memorandum and Articles of Association. A limited liability company enjoys perpetual existence unless its life is brought to an end through the prescribed ways as contained in the companies and Allied Matters Act 1990. The members (i.e. owners) of a limited company cannot be held individually responsible for the acts of the company as they are different from the company and they are usually not involved with the running of the affairs of the company. However, the directors and officers of the company may be held personally liable for the failure of the company, in certain circumstances, to comply with the provisions of the Companies and Allied Matters Act or the Memorandum and Articles of the Company. In essence, they could act "ultra vires" that is beyond their powers or beyond the powers of the company.

Let us now consider the factors that distinguish a private from a public limited company.

5.3.1 Private and Public Companies Compared

	Private Company	Public Company
Number of Shareholders	Minimum of two and maximum of fifty.	Minimum of Seven (7) and no maximum.
Transfer of Shares	Shares are not transferable as a private company is not quoted on the Stock Exchange.	Shares can be freely transferred because of Stock Exchange quotation.
Public Offer of Shares	Not allowed. Additional capital can be raised only from existing members. A private company is precluded from appealing to the public for capital.	Since there is no maximum number of shareholders, it can appeal to the public to raise additionalcapital i.e. to purchase its shares. It is therefore able to raise large sums of money to finance large-scale operations.

Number of Directors	Needs to have only one director.	Must have a minimum of two directors.
Retirement of Directors	Its directors may continue in office irrespective of age.	Directors retire after reaching certain age or after serving for a number of years. A retiring director could be re-elected by the approval of the shareholders at their meeting.

5.3.2 Formation of a Limited Company

The people who mute the idea of the formation of a limited company and see it through to incorporation and commencement of business/operation are called "promoters". The promoters are usually responsible for arranging the acquisition of land and/or building(s) and other property, drafting the Memorandum and Articles of Association, obtaining the consent of the first set of directors, registering the incorporation documents with the

Corporate Affairs Commission and paying the required fees for incorporation.

The following are the documents that must be submitted to the Registrar of Companies at the Corporate Affairs Commission by the promoters of a limited liability company.

(a) Memorandum of Association

(b) Articles of Association

(c) Particulars of Directors

(d) Registered Office of the Company

(e) Statement of Declaration of Compliance with registration requirements

The Registrar, if after screening the documents submitted, is satisfied that they are in order, will issue a Certificate of Incorporation to the company. From that date, the company comes into being as a new legal entity. Upon receiving the certificate of incorporation, a private company may immediately commence business whereas a public company must also obtain a Trading Certificate or a Certificate of Business before it can commence operation.

5.3.2.1 The Memorandum of Association

The Memorandum of Association is a document that determines the relationship between the company and outsiders. It contains matters of interest to people outside the company who may wish to deal with the company. This is because it is the document that states the nature of the business the company is allowed to engage in. An incorporated company is a legal entity but its capacity to do business is restricted unlike that of a real person. For instance, a company incorporated to buy and sell goods cannot embark on the manufacturing of such goods unless its objects clause is amended and registered with the Corporate Affairs Commission.

5.3.2.2 The Articles of Association

This document regulates the internal affairs of the company and the powers and duties of the directors. As an internal document, it also deals with matters such as procedure at meetings and the voting rights of different classes of shareholders, among others.

5.3.3   Limited Liability

An incorporated company must include the word "Limited" at the end of its name. The name of the company with the word "limited" must appear boldly outside its premises and on all documents used by it or issued to all the people having relationship with it. The principle of limited liability is to encourage investors to invest in the company as it assures them that they would not be required to make additional contributions to the loss of the company in excess of their agreed investment in the event of liquidation.

5.3.4 Control and Management of Limited Companies

The Management and Control of an incorporated company is vested, by the Articles of Association, on its directors. The directors exercise all the powers necessary for the conduct of the company's business. Where the directors intend to do anything not covered by the Articles, it is compulsory that the matter be brought before the shareholders at their meeting. The shareholders may then approve the alteration, after which it is registered at the Corporate Affairs Commission. This means that the shareholders control the directors.

In the same way that shareholders control the directors of a company, the directors in turn control the members of the company's management team by appointing a Managing Director or General Manager or President as Chief Executive Officer of the company.

5.3.5   Publication of Accounts

It is mandatory for a company to keep certain statutory books and records. These are:

(a) A register of members, with their names, addresses and shares held.

(b) A register of mortgages and charges on the company's assets.

(c) A register of Directors and Secretaries, with their names, addresses and shares held.

(d) Minute books for shareholders' and directors' meetings.

(e) Books of Accounts showing details of receipts and payments, assets and liabilities.

It is required that the accounts should show a true and fair view; otherwise the directors are liable to being sued for committing a criminal offence that can earn them a fine or imprisonment.

5.3.6   Liquidation

The life of a company is independent of and not tied to the survival of the individual shareholders that own it. As a separate legal person, a company is expected to exist perpetually. However, the corporate existence of a company can be brought to an end through the legal process of winding up or liquidation. This process involves converting the company's assets into cash for the purpose of paying the outstanding debts of the company, and distributing the surplus, if any, among its shareholders. Winding up or liquidation can take any of the following forms;

(a) Compulsory Liquidation: This occurs where the company is unable to pay its debts or is unable to fulfil its statutory obligations e.g. failure to commence business within one year or failure to hold statutory meeting; the court will then order a voluntary winding up if it feels that this process is just and equitable in the circumstance.

(b) Voluntary Winding Up: This   occurs where the company becomes insolvent. Voluntary winding up could be:

(i) Members' voluntary winding up, in which case the directors or a majority of them bring up a declaration of insolvency (and supports it by an affidavit) at a meeting of the board, and approved by a resolution of the shareholders at their meeting. The law requires that the directors must be sure that the company will be able to pay its debts in full from its assets within a specific period of time.

(ii) Creditors' Winding Up: This occurs where some creditors bring up an action against the company because of its inability to pay debts owed to them.

(c) Winding up subject to supervision of the court: This occurs where the court opts to protect members, creditors and even the company resulting from perceived fraud or irregularities in the voluntary winding up process. The court then issues an order enabling it to supervise the process. The liquidator appointed by the members or the creditors will therefore begin to report to the court until the winding up process is completed and he is discharged.

5.3.7 Advantages of Incorporation

Limited liability companies, by virtue of their corporate personality and size, possess a number of advantages. These are stated and discussed in the following paragraphs.

5.3.7.1 Continuity

The perpetual nature of existence of the limited liability company enables it to exist beyond the lives of its longest living owner. This gives greater confidence to its investors since the death of any shareholder, no matter how highly placed, could not bring the life of the company to an end.

5.3.7.2 Legal Being

An incorporated company, being a separate legal person, distinct from its owners, can sue and be sued in its own name, can own and dispose assets, and can incur liabilities. These provide protection for their owners who have agreed to engage in other businesses and are not required to answer for the company's actions. The owners of the company can also sue it where their rights are being infringed upon e.g. where an employee-shareholder is injured in the course of his employment; he has the right to sue the company.

5.3.7.2 Employment of Experts

The owners of an incorporated company are numerous and dispersed. Because they have invested their hard earned resources in the company, they will prefer to leave the management of the company in the hands of experts who are professionals and who possess the innovativeness and creative ability to utilize the company's resources to generate satisfactory returns for its numerous investors.

5.3.7.4 Limited Expansion

There is ample opportunity for a limited liability company to expand its capital, objectives, business activities and management simply by the passing of a resolution to amend the Memorandum and Articles of Association to reflect such expansion. In view of its ability to sell shares, a public company could increase the number of its shareholders and consequently its capital in several folds.

5.3.7.5 Ease of Ownership Transfer

The shares of a public company are easily transferred through the stock exchange market. A number of stockbrokers now exist to assist in this way. Also, one could sell his shares in a company and use that fund to buy shares in a company he adjudges to be better in the circumstance. This practice is known as investment switching.

5.3.8 Disadvantages of Incorporation

Despite the overwhelming advantages of a limited liability company, it also possesses the following disadvantages.

5.3.8.1 Bureaucracy

The members of the company must necessarily approve major decisions and actions. This entails time frame in view of the legal provision concerning statutory period of notice for the different types of the company's meetings.

5.3.8.2 Board Squabbles

This becomes frequent where one or a few board members decide to hold the company to Ransome because of their personal selfish interests.

5.3.8.3 High Cost of Incorporation

The cost of incorporation is high. This however depends on the amount of the company's authorized capital. To reduce cost, a company could be incorporated with a small amount of capital and increase it when its operation justifies/demands this increase.

5.3.8.4 Higher Rate of Tax

The company pays tax on its profits. The rate of tax is usually higher than that paid by individuals. Also, the distributable profits of the company (dividends) are taxed in the hands of each shareholder. This further increases the tax paid on the returns on the investment of every investor.

5.4   International Companies

An international company is one that sells its goods and services across national boundaries i.e. a company that engages in international trade.

An international company has to comply with the legal, political social, cultural, economic and technological requirements of the different countries in which it trades. It must also adjust to the business practices, institutions and competitive activities in those countries in addition to complying with quality, pricing, advertising, packaging and other standards required of his product(s) in those countries.

A company could become international through any of the following:

(a) Exporting to other countries, even if it is to a single customer, on a regular basis.

(b) Appointing a representative or agent to sell on its behalf in another country.

(c) Setting up a sales office to handle the sales of its products in other countries.

An international company necessarily earns foreign currency that converts to the local currency. Internationalizing a company is usually done to exploit the opportunities in foreign markets to sell surplus goods and to earn higher profits than would be earned by concentrating in the home market alone.

5.5 Multinational Company

A multinational company is one which has a direct investment base (manufacturing or service operation) in one or more countries and in which policy decisions are based on alternatives available anywhere in the world.

According to L.S. Walsh, the objectives of a multinational company are to:

(a) Maximize the operating performance of the individual units by making available the resources of the company's headquarters in terms of management expertise, technical knowhow, financial assets, market intelligence, etc;

(b) Minimize the problems that arise from distance between operating units and from diversity of operating conditions and personnel, e.g. the exercise of too much or too little initiative, or actions taken with inadequate knowledge of the local market;

(c) Co-ordinate the activities of individual companies where these are interdependent.

Multinational companies usually need to incorporate a company with the same name in all the countries in which they operate, e.g. Mobil Oil Incorporation of the United States of America is Mobil Oil Nigeria Plc in Nigeria.

5.6   The Co-operative Society

A co-operative society is an association or organisation of people who have agreed to come together for a common purpose. The most common form of co-operative society is the Credit and Thrift Co-operative Society (CTCS). There are Farmers' Co-operative Societies, the Co-operative Supply Associations, Traders' Co-operative Societies, Transporters' Co-operative Societies, etc, established along functional or service lines. There are also co-operative unions for different types of purposes. A co-operative union is a conglomeration of many co-operative societies.

The co-operative movements in the South-West and South-East of Nigeria led to the establishment of Co-operative Bank Plc and the Co-operative Development Bank Plc.

5.6.1   Characteristics of Co-operative Societies

No matter the type or nature of the various co-operative societies in existence, they have the same features, which are;

5.6.1.1 Purpose

Every co-operative society is formed to cater for the interest of members. Each society is formed for a specific purpose e.g. Credit and Thrift, Essential Commodities, Farming, Trading, Transportation, etc.

5.6.1.2 Ownership and Capital

The capital of the society is called shares and is contributed by members. These members are owners of the society. There is no limit to the maximum number of members a society could have; membership thus depends on agreement between the existing members who may decide to admit more members or restrict further admission of new members for some time.

5.6.1.3 Management

The management of a co-operative society is usually in the hands of a management committee chosen by election at the inaugural meeting of the society or at subsequent annual general meetings. Each management committee is technically elected to serve for a year but any member of the committee may be re-elected upon satisfactory performance for as long as the society may wish.

5.6.1.4 Voting Right

Every member is entitled to one vote irrespective of the number of shares he holds in the society. A member's voting right cannot be transferred, as voting by proxy is not allowed.

5.6.1.5 Share of Profit

The profit of a co-operative society is shared by members, not in accordance with capital contribution, but on the basis of patronage. For instance, in a credit society, a member who took more loans is likely to earn greater dividend than one who took no loan at all.

5.6.2 Control of Co-operative Societies

The Ministry of Co-operatives in any state (sometimes Trade and Co-operatives or Industries and Co-operatives) controls the activities of all the co-operative societies in the State. This is done through the Registrar of Co-operatives and his team of Co-operative Inspectors. The Registrar registers all the co-operative societies in a state and issues them with a Certificate of Registration/Incorporation and Bye Laws.

5.7 Public Corporations

These are companies established by the government for the purpose of providing public utilities to the people and to enhance the level of economic development. The main aim of establishing public corporations is not to make profit but to provide certain goods and services that would normally have been out of the reach of the people because of cost, size, technology and some other considerations. However, public corporations need to be run on commercial basis in order to enable them to provide efficient services and replace their worn out or obsolete assets, thus being able to continue to provide the goods or services for which they are established on a continuing basis. Examples of public corporations in Nigeria include: the Central Bank of Nigeria, the Nigerian Railway Corporation, the Nigeria Airways, the National Aviation Handling Company, The Bulk Purchasing Corporations of various states, the National Electric Power Authority, the various State's Water Corporation and Housing Corporation, the National maritime Authority, the Nigeria Ports Authority, the Nigerian Postal Services, the Nigerian Telecommunications Company, etc.

5.7.1   Reasons for Public Corporations

As stated above, public corporations are designed to satisfy the welfare needs of the people and help to accelerate the level of economic development. Specifically, the essence of Public Corporations can be discussed under the following headings:

5.7.1.1 To Satisfy Public Need

The citizens of a country need certain goods and services, which cannot be left in the hands of the private sector if the government is not to sacrifice the welfare of its citizens for private interests.

Examples here include the provision of roads, health and educational services, the building of airports and waterways, the provision of pipe borne water, power supply, etc.

5.7.1.2 Peculiar Nature of Some Services

The peculiar nature of some services encourages the establishment of public corporations in order to ensure there is sanity in the economy. For instance, the government owes it a duty to ensure that every citizen enjoys equal treatment in the provision of social amenities anywhere the citizens may be in the country without any marked difference in the price paid to enjoy those amenities and irrespective of the number of people residing in a particular location. If such services are left in the hands of private investors, they will concentrate on areas/locations with sufficient number of customers that would justify a quick payback and adequate return on investment. Some towns and villages, for instance, would not have been linked by road, electricity, telecommunications and other networks if these services were to be left in the hands of the private sector operators who will consider viability before extending such services to any location.

5.7.1.3 Huge Capital Investment

The huge capital investment required to provide certain utilities is prohibitive for the private sector to raise. Related to this is the long gestation period of such projects e.g. the building of an airport, a new capital city, provision of broadcasting services, etc

5.7.1.4 Efficiency in the Allocation of Scarce Resources

The establishment of public corporations to provide services like water, electricity, rail services, etc. is the way to avoid unnecessary duplication and ultimately to ensure that the scarce economic resources of a nation are efficiently allocated. For instance, one can only imagine the problems associated with three or four companies supplying water to a single town. Imagine the ways pipes would cross each other as they strive to outdo one another.

5.7.2   Problems of Public Corporations

Public corporations, it has been generally agreed, have not lived up to the expectation of the people in most countries. The reasons for this are summarized in the following paragraphs.

5.7.2.1 Their Aims have been difficult to define

"Satisfying public interest" which appears to be the objective of most public corporations appears too vague as to connote any meaning, even to the managers of these corporations. Some corporations are now required to generate revenue comparable to that achievable in the private sector but without the freehand and adequate resources to do this. Thus, their managers get confused and pursue other goals rather than work to satisfy public interest.

5.7.2.2 Government Interference

Once established, the government is not expected to interfere with the operations of these corporations. There are always instruments establishing these corporations. The instrument could be an Act of Parliament or decree. Whatever it is, it normally states the purpose, aims and objectives, organisation structure and management, sources of capital, quality of employees, among others.

What happens in practice is that often the right people are not employed to man these organisations. Most of the time, board members are political appointees who many not have any faint idea about business, management, etc. and who may not be specialists in the field of service of the corporation. Since the headship determines the composition of the body to a large extent, a mediocre head, will like to recruit his own "yes men" and political sycophants and stooges to work with him. The result is usually inefficiency and wastages of taxpayers' fund.

5.7.2.3 Lack of Accountability

Most public corporations do not prepare annual accounts. Where these are prepared, they may come many years after the headship had been changed. The accounts of these corporations are sometimes also not subjected to external audit. Over the years, there have been no public fora to call managers of these bodies to question but the situation may soon change as more and more people become enlightened about the fact that public corporations are set up from the financial resources of our country or state, which could have been put into better alternative uses.

5.7.2.4 Persistent Losses

Most public corporations have suffered persistent losses meaning colossal waste of the hard earned financial resources of the state, which are supposed to be efficiently and effectively managed by the government to whom they have been entrusted.

5.7.2.5 Inefficiency

Most public corporations have not provided the services they are established to provide in an efficient manner. For instance, how can one explain enjoying water supply one day in a month and one is made to pay a full month's rate? This is paying for inefficiency and one can hardly help the situation because there is no competition.

5.7.2.6 The Protective Laws Governing their Existence

The laws establishing these corporations give them the power of natural monopoly and they cannot be taken to the law courts. The result is that they are not responsive to criticisms, neither are they sensitive to the yearnings and aspirations of the people they serve.

It is for the above reasons that some public corporations are now being commercialized while some are privatized. The government is also encouraging competition in some areas in order to avoid cases where the economy or the citizens will be put in jeopardy.

5.8   Non-Governmental Organisations (NGOs)

These are private non-profit making organisations established for the common good of the people. There are large numbers of these organisations today. Each of them provides a unique service. There are some whose main purpose or aim is to enlighten people and encourage them to embrace democracy; some are concerned with health e.g. – guinea worm eradication; eradication of river blindness, polio, etc; some others are concerned with how to better the lot of the less privileged, the motherless, the handicap, etc;

there are some others which exist for the purpose of protecting people from human rights abuse. Some examples of NGOs include:

(a) Campaign for Democracy (CD)

(b) Children in Distress Bureau (CIDB)

(c) Committee Against Child Abuse and Neglect (CACAN)

(d) Consumer Rights Forum (CRF)

(e) The Save Accident Victims Association of Nigeria (CAVAN)

(f) The Royal Advancement for Development (RADEV)

(g) Akiode Foundation and Education Help Initiative (EHIN)

While some NGOs are local in outlook, some operate internationally.

Every NGO must have a constitution which spells out its aims and objectives, sources of funds, mode of operation, the people behind its establishment, contact addresses, programs and projects, etc.

Chapter Six

RAISING CAPITAL FOR BUSINESS

6.0   Capital and Assets

These are two important and indispensable aspects of business. Depending on the way the capital is described, it can be converted to assets while both could mean the same thing sometimes. The following discussion on both terms will elucidate these assertions more.

6.1   Capital

The term capital can mean different things to different people. While some business people believe it is money, economists call it real wealth i.e goods that can be kept and used over and over again. It is the feeling of business people that money is used to obtain these goods that economists talk about and this is their justification for equating capital with money.

L.Gartside mentions that capital can be employed in business in two quite different senses.

(a)   As one of the indispensable agents of modern production, consisting of buildings, equipment, etc and

(b)   As the stock of money used for carrying on a business

The first of these two accords with the view of economists while the second is in agreement with the position of business people.

In whatever way capital is defined, it is necessary for anybody doing business or intending to do business to give the issue of capital good thought as it is with it that other business resource (land, building, machinery, equipment, labor, the services of consultants, etc.) are acquired for the proper running of a business. Capital must be adequate at all times to keep the wheel of business moving and to reduce stress usually faced by business people when they experience temporary shortage of capital.

6.2   Assets

These are the resources or the property and possessions owned by a business. Assets are usually categorized into fixed and current. Fixed assets are those tangible assets which are used in a business for a longtime and which cannot be sold quickly without affecting the normal business activities of the organisations. The value of any fixed asset is depreciated or amortized over its useful life. The charge for the use or replacement of such asset is called Depreciation or Amortization. Examples of such assets are land and buildings, motor vehicles,, plant and machinery, furniture and fittings, etc. Current assets are those assets that can be easily realized for the purpose of discharging liabilities e.g.

stock-in-trade, debtors, bills receivable and cash in hand and at bank. Assets could also be tangible or intangible. Tangible assets are those physical assets, which can be seen or touched while intangible assets cannot be seen or touched e.g. goodwill, trademark, patent right, etc.

6.3   Types of Capital

There are different types of capital. We shall consider the following types:

(a) Fixed Capital

(b) Circulating Capital

(c) Working Capital

(d) Loan/Debt Capital

(e) Long term Capital

(f) Short term Capital

(g) Equity Capital

(h) Permanent Capital

6.3.1   Fixed Capital

This is used to describe that part of capital of a business, which can be used for a number of times over a long period of time with replacement only being done after a fairly long internal. The fixed assets of a business organisation fall into the following category.

6.3.2   Circulating Capital

This is the capital that is used once and then replenished on a continuing basis through the normal operations of a business e.g. raw material is used up and a new stock of it is bought to enable the company to continue in production or in business. The value or amount of circulating capital keeps changing; sometimes cash on hands is banked, the position changes, if the raw material increases for the time being. When the raw material is processed into finished goods and sold, cash is again generated. The current assets of a business are its circulating capital because their values change when a transaction involving them occurs.

6.3.3   Working Capital

The amount which a business organisation utilizes for the running of its affairs after the acquisition of fixed assets is its working capital. This can be described as the excess of current assets over current liabilities in a business in continuous operation (i.e. a going concern). Working capital is very important for the survival of any business organisation, be it manufacturing, agriculture, distribution, health, education or hotel services.

6.3.4 Loan/Debt Capital

The portion of the fixed or working capital of a business organisation, which it has borrowed, is referred to as loan or debt capital. The borrowing could be in the form of overdraft, term loan, commercial paper, debenture stock etc. The proportion of a company's loan or debt capital determines its gearing level. A company loan is said to be highly geared if it carries a high proportion of loan or debt in its capital structure. It is low geared if the loan portion of the total capital is low.

6.3.5 Long term Capital

This is represented by that part of a company's capital which remains in the business for a long term, it is made up of the owners' contribution and long term loan. Since it is agreed that the capital invested in a company is loan to that company which it is bound to repay to its owners, we can safely say that all long term capital is loan capital. However, not all loan capital is long term capital. The components of long term capital include debenture, loan stock, mortgage and term loans.

6.3.6   Short term Capital

That part of the capital of a business organisation which is only available for a short term is called short term capital. Since technically, capital is loan and is expected to be repaid, short term capital can be described as money borrowed by a business which is due for repayment within a short period of time. Some of the components of short term capital include bank overdraft, invoice discounting, trade credit, commercial paper, and bankers' acceptance.

6.3.7   Equity Capital

This is the amount invested in a business by the ordinary shareholders together with any undistributed (i.e. retained) earning of the business. Losses will reduce the equity capital while profits will increase it. This is so because profits and losses belong to the owners of the business.

6.3.8   Permanent Capital

The ordinary shares of a company represent its permanent capital. The reason for this is that even though the capital of a company constitutes a loan as the business continues to run. In a public limited company however, any shareholder could sell his/her shareholding by selling his shares through the Stock Exchange Market. Many stockbrokers are now in business to help facilitate the sale of such shares.

6.4   Sources of Capital

In whatever way capital can be defined, it can be raised from two main sources:

(a) Internal Sources

(b) External Sources.

6.4.1   Internal Sources of Capital

These are sources from which a company or business raise capital within the organisation, we will discuss the following sources under this heading:

(a) The capital account

(b) Retained Earnings

(c) Right Issues

(d) Sales of Assets

(e) Sale and Lease Back

6.4.1.1 The Capital Account

Fund is provided for the start up and running of a business, whether it is a sole proprietorship, partnership or limited liability company. Such fund, to the extent that it is provided by the owners of the business (including the amount paid in exchange for the shares of a company), represents the capital of the business and is thus provided from the internal sources of the business. There is usually no complication in the capital accounts of the sole proprietorship and partnership business but the capital account of a limited company is replete with complications in that it is important to distinguish between authorized, normal, registered, called-up, issued, subscribed, paid-up, uncalled and unissued capital. The share capital of a company could also be made up of ordinary or preference shares and the variant of these.

Authorized Capital: is the maximum amount of capital, which the company intends to raise for its operation and it is usually stated in the memorandum of association. Stamp duty is paid on this amount to the Registrar of Companies at the Corporate Affairs Commission. The authorized capital can be amended as the company's operation expands but this has to be approved at a meeting of the shareholders of the company. The new authorized capital must also be registered with the Corporate Affairs Commission. Another name for authorized capital is Registered capital because it is the amount of capital with which the company was registered.

Nominal Capital:　　This is the unit value of the shares of a company multiplied by the number of shares. For instance, if the authorized capital of a company is 100,000 ordinary shares of N1:00 while the nominal capital is N1 in one hundred thousand places which equals N100,000. This is different from the market price/value of the shares of the company. The market price may be lower or higher than the nominal price. When it is lower, the shares of the company are said to be selling at a discount and at a premium when it is higher.

Called-Up Capital: This represents the portion of the issued or authorized capital of a company which the shareholders have been requested to pay. A company is not required to raise the whole of the registered capital at once. The company may decide that it would be raised instalmentally e.g. in four installments. Each installment is a "call", thus the term "called up capital.

Issued Capital: Shares can only be paid for, when they are issued by the company, that portion of capital issued and for which shareholders are asked to subscribe is the "issued capital". The portion of the issued capital which has been subscribed for (i.e. paid for) is the subscribed capital.

Paid-Up Capital: This is the total amount already paid in consideration for shares in a company by the shareholders. It may be different from the called-up or issued capital where part of this is yet to be paid by the subscribers. The amount unpaid is usually referred to as "calls in arrears" or "calls unpaid".

Uncalled Capital: This is that part of the nominal or issued capital for which subscribers have not been requested to make the payment.

Unissued Capital: is the portion of the shares of the company, which has not been issued for subscription at all.

Share Capital: The share capital of a company represents the investment of the shareholders in that company. A share is a unit (or the individual portion) of that investment. A shareholder could own as many shares as he has the financial capacity to buy subject to limitations in the Memorandum or Articles of Associations and provisions of the Companies and Allied Matters Act. There are two main classes of shares: Ordinary and Preference.

Ordinary Shares: These are shares which entitle their holders to control the company through voting to appoint directors and take other decisions like change in the authorized capital, change in the nature/line of business of the company and such other major changes or decisions e.g. major borrowing for the company's operation. The ordinary shareholders are the risk bearers of the company and for that they are entitled to the profits of the company. The profit of a company is distributed as dividends based on the number of the shareholding in the company. In the event of a loss, the shareholders do not receive any reward (dividend) for their investment.

Preference Shares: These are shares, which entitle its holders to have a prior claim on the profits of the company. The claim of preference shareholders is usually a fixed percentage e.g. 5% preference shares means the shareholders will receive annual reward of 5% of whatever they have invested in the company. Preference shares are not commonly issued in Nigeria.

6.4.1.2 Retained Earnings

This is profit not distributed to the shareholders in the form of dividends. For as long as the profit remains undistributed, it is available for use in the business (i.e. retained in the business). If there is a deliberate decision to return or plough back part of the profits of a business, the effect is to increase the capital account of the owners of the business. In the case of companies, wherever profit is to be retained permanently in the business, the amount of profit is capitalized by the issue of bonus shares to the shareholders in the proportion of their shareholding in the company.

6.4.1.3   Rights Issue

Apart from the initial share issues, a company may decide to issue new shares at a price lower than the existing market price to existing shareholders to encourage them to increase their shareholding in the company. This method of raising capital and this class of shares is called "Rights Issue".

6.4.1.4 Sale of Assets

A company in need of operational funds could sell some of its redundant assets for cash. This will help to relieve the company of financial stress in the meantime and the returns generated by the new fund injection could be used to acquire modern assets that could be used to further improve the business of the organisation.

6.4.1.5 Sale and Lease Back

Instead of an outright sale, a company could even sell some of its active assets and lease them back for its operations. This method affords the company the continued use of that asset and some operational funds at the same time. The cost paid by the company for the lease of the assets could be offset from increased revenue earnings generated from the cash received from the sale of the assets, which it has now leased.

6.4.2 External Sources of Capital

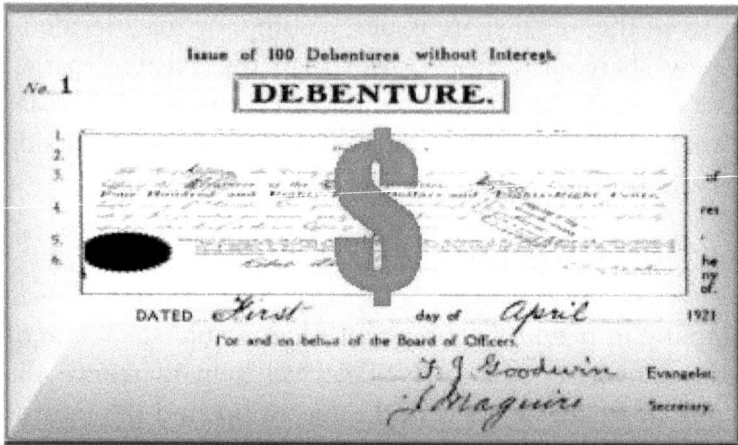

There are various external sources from which a company could raise capital. These include:

(a) Debentures

(b) Loans

(c) Mortgages

(d) Trade Credit

(e) Overdrafts

(f) Sale of Debts/Factoring

(g) Acceptance Credits

(h) Invoice Discounting

(i) Equipment Leasing

(j) Hire Purchase

(k) Commercial Papers

A major characteristic of external sources of capital is that one form of collateral security or another is required for most of the listed options. Collateral security is some form of asset that can be sold to provide money to repay the amount of money borrowed for running the affairs of the company in case of failure to repay as agreed.

6.4.2.1   Debentures

A debenture is a loan to an incorporated company by investors at a fixed or determinable rate of interest. In essence a debenture is a certificate of indebtedness issued by a company to investors who have lent money to it. Debentures are divided into small units like shares but debenture-holders are only creditors to the company and not owners as in the case of shareholders. Like shares, debentures may also be transferable i.e. debentures may also be traded at the stock exchange. Debentures are issued for a fixed term and interest is paid whether the company makes profit or not. A debenture which is secured by a charge on the assets of the company, which has issued it is called Mortgage Debenture. Where no assets are charged, it means the debenture is unsecured. Such a debenture is called Simple or Naked Debenture. A debenture could be redeemable or irredeemable. It is redeemable if it has a fixed determinable date or repayment. Where there is no date of repayment, except in the case of default of payment of interest, the debenture is said to be irredeemable. Debentures could also be convertible, that is may be converted to ordinary shares at a determinable date. It should be noted that failure to pay interest when due or to observe the terms of the debenture issue entitles the debenture-holders the right to appoint a Receiver who would take over the control of the company from shareholders on their behalf (i.e. debenture holders).

6.4.2.2   Loans

Secured and unsecured loans from banks, other financial institutions and institutional investors are now a common occurrence. There are also development financial institutions, which are established by the government for the purpose of providing the necessary funding for different types of businesses. Some of these development finance institutions include the Nigerian Industrial Development Bank (NIDB), Nigerian Bank for Commerce and Industry (NBCI), National Economic Reconstruction Fund

(NERFUND) and the Nigerian-Export-Import Bank (NEXIM). NIDB and NBCI have both been collapsed into one institution now known as the Bank of Industry (BOI).

6.4.2.3   Mortgages

This is an arrangement whereby a company uses its land, or property to borrow money while still occupying the property until it completes repayment of the loan.

6.4.2.4 Trade Credit

When a company delays the payment of amounts owed to other companies and individuals, such a company is said to be enjoying trade credit. The credit is usually arranged between the company and its creditors while in some circumstances trade credit arises out of custom of trade. Whatever form trade credit takes, it is usually at a cost.

6.4.2.5   Overdrafts

A short-term credit facility to a company or individual by a bank in which a customer keeps a current account is called an overdraft. Overdraft is a common source of working capital for companies. It is a simple method of raising capital. It operates simply by seeking the bank's authority to enable a customer to overdraw the amount in the current account.

6.4.2.6   Factoring/Sale of Debts

A company in dire need of funds could sell some of its debts to a factor. The factor agrees to pay a reduced amount of the debt sold to it. The difference between the amount of the debt and the amount paid by the factor is factor's commission or fee. The factor gains this amount when he collects the debt from **the** company's debtors.

6.4.2.7 Acceptance Credits

This is otherwise known as bill finance. The bill could be a bill of exchange or a promissory note. Bills of exchange and promissory notes are usually post-dated for between 30 and 180days. They are issued by vendors and sent to their customers, to whom they intend to advance credit, to accept the terms contained in the document by signing his signature on it. Once accepted the bill of exchange or promissory note becomes a financial instrument that evidences the amount of credit that a seller has granted to a buyer over a stated period of time. Whilst the bill of exchange is common in international trade, the promissory note is issued in local trade. The creditor or holder of the bill could also discount it to raise fund for his operation.

Create Invoices

Previous Next Spelling History Journal

Customer:Job
Beach Bike

Class
Salt Lake...

Template Print Preview
Copy of: Intuit Produc

Invoice

Date 05/05/2009   Invoice # 3

Bill To
Beach Bike
555 Suntan Ave.
Santa Barbara, CA 93101
UNITED STATES

Ship To
Beach Bike
555 Suntan Ave.
Santa Barbara, CA 93101
UNITED STATES

P.O. Number	Terms	Rep	Ship	Via	F.O.B.
	COD		05/05/2009	Will Call	Origin

Quantity	Item	Item Code	Description	UOM	Price Each	Amount	Tax
1	B202	FB_Item	B202 - Everyday Brake Cables	ea	14.25	14.25	Tax
		FB_Discoun...	10% Discount		-10.0%	-1.43	Tax

Customer Message

Tax Utah (6.7%)   0.86
Total   13.68

☑ To be printed
☐ To be e-mailed

Add Time/Costs...   Apply Credits...
Customer Tax Code Tax

Payments Applied   0.00
Balance Due   13.68

Memo FB: SO# - 50031.

Learn about our payment processing and online invoicing solutions.

Save & Close   Save & New   Revert

6.4.2.8   Invoice Discounting

This method is adopted to improve liquidity. Instead of the debt being sold outright as in the case of factoring, the documents evidencing a debt are presented to professional financiers who agree to discount the bills by paying the company a reduced amount (a discounted amount) pending the time that the debtor pays the amount owing to the company. When the debt is received, the company now pays over the whole amount to the financier.

6.4.2.9 Equipment Leasing

This is another form of finance. A company could lease equipment for its use and pay rental charges over a period of time for the use of the asset. There are different types of leasing. While some confer ownership on the lessee upon taking up the lease, others ensure that the lessor retains ownership until when the financial installment of the rent is paid. Some other lease arrangements only allow the use of the asset in consideration for the payment of rentals; there is no purchase option. A company could also arrange to sell an asset to raise fund and lease the asset back from the buyer. This is known as sale and lease back. This arrangement affords the company the opportunity of raising working capital by selling a useful asset and still gains the use of the asset. Sometimes the option to own the asset after full payment of rental charges and purchase fees by the lessee is incorporated into the agreement.

6.4.2.10   Hire Purchase

This is like leasing but the option to purchase is compulsory except when the hirer defaults in the payment of hire charges. In such a case, the vendor can repossess the asset.

6.4.2.11   Commercial Paper

This is a source open to blue chip companies to raise short term fund. The company issues commercial paper for the amount required and a financial intermediary helps to source investors in the commercial paper. The commercial paper is usually an unsecured credit and this is the reason why it is issued by established and well-known companies which are not likely to default in payment when the instrument falls due for redemption. Commercial papers are issued for between 30 and 180 days at a rate very close to the commercial rate of interest. A large number of commercial papers contain the roll over option i.e. the possibility of renewal for one or more terms. For instance, a 30-day paper could be rolled over for another 30 days and then for a further 30 days. Each roll over may attract higher rate of interest.

Chapter Seven

BUSINESS ETHICS

7.0   What is ethics?

thics is a set moral principle while ethics is a set of principles and rules of conduct – Cassell Paperback Dictionary (New Edition).

Ethics is the discipline dealing with what is good and with moral duty and obligation – Webster's Ninth New Collegiate Dictionary.

From the foregoing, ethics is concerned with the "dos" and "don'ts" in a particular society, within a group of people or in an organisation. It shapes the behaviour pattern in the group, society or an organisation. It therefore means that ethics is not only relevant in business, but it is applicable to governments, Universities, political organisation, social group, cultural organisations, etc. In fact, it is applicable anywhere managing is done.

7.1   Types of Ethics

The fact that ethics is applicable to all spheres of life means that there can be different types of ethics. Here, we shall consider only four types, which are: personal, accounting, marketing and business.

Personal ethics refers to the rules by which an individual lives his/her personal life. Personal ethics cover issues such as what, when and where to eat e.g. some people do not eat outside, some are vegetarians, and some have rigid eating times; what to wear; who to relate or associate with and the degree of relationship and association.

Accounting ethics is the code that guides the professional conduct of accountants. Marketing ethics refer to the code of ethics guiding the conduct of professional marketers. The code of ethics for members of the Institute of Chartered Accountants of Nigeria, and the Chartered Institute of

Marketing, London, are included at the end of this chapter for useful reference.

Business ethics is a more general term as it covers all area of business and those areas sharing any relationship with business. In the words of Weihrich and Koontz, business ethics is concerned with truth and justice and has a variety of aspects such as the expectation of the society, fair competition, advertising, public relations, social responsibilities, consumer autonomy, and corporate behaviour in the home country as well as abroad. The scope of business ethics is wide and calls for study and understanding by all business people.

7.2   Ethical Theories

There basic types of theories have been developed to analyse and understand ethics. These are: utilitarian theory, theory of right and theory of justice.

Utilitarian theory suggests that plans and actions should be evaluated in terms of their consequences or outcomes. The idea behind this is that these should produce the greatest good for the greatest number of people. Thus, where certain plans and actions are not designed for the good of the generality of members of an organisation, group, community or society, it is not utilitarian, it is unfair and it is undesirable.

The theory of rights holds that all people have basic rights e.g. rights to freedom of conscience, free speech, education, living, etc. This suggests that every code of ethics must aim to protect the fundamental rights of those who subscribe to it in accordance with the provisions of constitutions of the country or countries where the group operates. Note that every country has a section of dealing with Fundamental Human Rights in its constitution.

The theory of justice demands that decision makers should be guided by fairness and equity, as well as impartiality. This will ensure justice and fair play and will give every member of the society, group, association or organisation a sense of belonging as they will have confidence in their leaders and in their power and ability to judge without fair of favor.

7.3   Institutionalizing Ethics

The aim or purpose of institutionalizing ethics is to ensure that every member of the organisation is aware of and conforms to the ethics of the organisation. It is important to create an environment that fosters ethical decision-making by institutionalizing ethics in any organisation, group or society. The responsibility for this rests squarely on the managers or leaders. Leaders and managers must not only create the enabling environment, they must be committed to upholding ethical standards within their areas of jurisdiction.

They can achieve these by applying and integrating ethical concepts in their daily actions.

The following methods can be adopted to ensure that ethics is institutionalized in any society, group or organisation, and that it permeates the entire establishment, whether business, government, religion, etc;

(a) By using/establishing an appropriate company policy or a code of ethics, which is published for the knowledge of all.

(b) By using a formally appointed ethics committee which saddled with the task of reviewing, implementing, communicating and enforcing the organisation's code of ethics. The specific functions of an ethics committee would include the following:

(1) Holding regular meetings to discuss ethical issues

(2) Ensuring that ethics are well understood by all members of the organisation.

(3) Communicating the code to all members of the organisation

(4) Checking for possible violations of the code

(5) Enforcing the code

(6) Rewarding compliance and punishing violations

(7) Reviewing and updating the code, and

(8) Reporting activities of the committee to the board of directors.

(c) By teaching ethics in management development programs organized within and outside the organisation.

7.4   Code of Ethics

A code is a statement of policies, principles, or rules that guides behavior. Codes of ethics are now available to guide the behaviour of persons in organized set ups and in everyday life. There is a Code of Conduct Bureau in Nigeria, which has established a code for all civil servants. There is also the anti-graft law to punish those who violate the provisions of the code by corruptly enriching themselves and engaging in such other sharp and unwholesome practices. Reference has earlier been made to the code of professional ethics for members of the Institute of Chartered Accountants of Nigeria and the Chartered Institute of Marketing, London.

7.5   Ethical Standards

Ethical standards differ among business organisations, government, professional bodies, social organisations, communities, etc. For instance, while payments to government officials and other people with political influences to court their favor in handling transactions may not be regarded as bribes but as necessary and proper payments for services rendered in some countries, it may be a criminal offence in some other countries. Despite the fact that this type of practice is offensive in Nigeria, many people have regarded it as a normal and acceptable way of doing business and this is the reason government contracts are not perfectly executed or not executed at all by those who won the contracts. Also, while it is unacceptable to give bribe to obtain government contracts in the United States of America, it is a societal norm to give tips at restaurants.

It is important to uphold ethical standards in any society or organisation. This has the potential of reducing conflicts and ensuring peaceful co-existence. The upholding and maintenance of standards in an organisation will serve as a motivation for improving existing standards and introducing new forms of ethics which would in turn help to improve the quality of life in such an organisation or society.

The following factors have been suggested as means of raising ethical standards:

(1) Disclosure and publicity of ethical standards

(2) Formal means of educating all concerned about the ethics of the society or organisation.

(3) Objective enforcement of ethics. Unethical managers should be held responsible for their actions. This means that privileges and benefits should be withdrawn and sanctions should be applied. Enforcement of ethical codes may not be easy but the mere existence of such codes can increase ethical behaviour and compliance. Objective enforcement also suggests impartiality in punishing non-compliance.

(4) Support from top management as well as top management compliance with the ethical code. The code should be no respecter of any person.

(5) Providing clear guidelines for ethical behaviour.

(6) Conducting frequent and unpredictable audits.

(7) Ensuring that loyalty to the company does not constitute an excuse for improper behaviour or actions. Loyalty is not synonymous with compliance.

Chapter Eight

SOCIAL RESPONSIBILITY

8.0   Social Responsibility Defined

It has been proved beyond reasonable doubt that the main aim of doing business is to make profit. Thus, every business has an economic motive. It has also been confirmed that no business can succeed if it fails to recognize societal problems and be part of the solution process. This means that active participation in solving certain problems in the environment is the function of the manager. The modern trend is that managers are being asked by society to contribute more to the environment in which they do business.

Social responsibility has been defined as "the act of making conscious effort at ensuring that the company's action impact positively on society". Defined in this way, social responsibility therefore, is applicable not only to business organisation but also to governments, churches, schools, non-governmental organisations, charitable organizations, and social clubs. All these need to impact positively on the society. It can be said with high degree of assurance that organisations that are not socially responsible are unlikely to succeed in the future.

8.1   Social Responsiveness

This is a newly developed concept and has close similarity to social responsibility. It is the ability of an organisation to relate its operation and policies to the social environment in ways that are mutually beneficial to the organisation and the society. Social responsibility and social responsiveness have become interchangeable terms in modern management thinking and business practice.

8.2   Social Responsibility and Business

The following summarizes arguments for and against the involvement of business organisations in social activities. The summary is culled from Management: A Global Perspective (Tenth Edition) by Weihrich and Koontz, published by McGraw Hill International Editions. The original work belongs to Frederick Davis and Post based on their text. Business and Society (6th Edition) by McGraw-Hill Book Company, New York.

8.2.1   Arguments for Social Involvement of Business

1.   Public needs have changed, leading to changed expectations. Business, it is suggested, received its charter from society and consequently has to respond to the needs of society.

2.   The creation of a better social environment benefits both society and business. Society gains through better neighborhoods and

employment applications; business benefits from a better community, since the community is the source of its work force and the consumer of its product and services.

3. Social involvement discourages additional government regulation and intervention. The result is greater freedom and more flexibility in decision making for business.

4. Business has great deal of power that, it is reasoned, should be accompanied by an equal amount of responsibility.

5. Modern society is an interdependent system, and the internal activities of the enterprise have an impact on the external environment.

6. Social involvement may be in the interest of stockholders.

7. Problems can become profits. Items that may once have been considered waste (for example, empty soft drink cans) can be profitably used again.

8.   Social involvement creates a favorable public image. Thus, a firm may attract customers, employees and investors.

9.   Business should try to solve the problems that other institutions have not been able to solve. After all, business has a history of coming up with moral ideas.

10.   Business has the resources. Specifically, business should use its talented managers and specialists, as well as its capital resources, to solve some of society's problems.

11.   It is better to prevent social problems through business involvement than to cure them. It may be easier to help the hard-core unemployment than to cope with social unrest.

8.2.2   Arguments against Social Involvement of Business

1.   The primary task of business is to maximize profit by focusing strictly on economic activities. Social involvement could reduce economic efficiency.

2. In final analysis, society must pay for the social involvement of business organisations and this would create excessive costs for business, which cannot commit its resources to social action.

3. Social involvement can create a weakened international balance of payments situation. The cost of social programs, the reasoning goes, would have to be added to the price of the product. Thus, companies selling in international markets would be at a disadvantage when competing with companies in other countries that do not have these social costs to hear. (This case is more pertinent to Nigeria, where the degree of expectation of social responsibility and social involvement from companies is quite high).

4. Business has encouraged power, and additional social involvement would further increase its power and influence.

5. Business people lack the social skills to deal with problems of society. Their training and experience is with economic matters, and their skills may not be pertinent to social problems.

6.   There is lack of accountability of business to society. Unless accountability can be established, business should not get involved.

7.   There is not complete support for involvement in social actions. Consequently, disagreements among groups with different viewpoints will cause friction.

In some societies, for example in the Niger Delta area of Nigeria, the society no longer look unto governments (locals, state and national) for development and provision of social amenities, they have shifted a high degree of responsibility to the organisations operating within their area, forgetting completely that these organisations are primarily set for profit and that they pay tax to the government, which in turn should provide the required amenities. This is the major source of conflict between Shell and the Ogonis in Rivers State, Mobil and the people of Akwa Ibom State, Shell and the Ijaw Youths in Bayelsa and Delta States.

The people of the Niger Delta should understand that 'Rome

was not built in a day' and that development is a gradual process. Business organisations operating within their area should be allowed undisturbed operations so that they can realize their business motive and plough back some of the profits earned into social service provision. It could be agreed for these organitions to contribute a certain percentage of their annual profits to an environmental social development fun which should be managed by a board of trustee. It is believed that this will support the Niger Delta Development Commission (NDDC) recently established by Olusegun Obasanjo's government and allow for faster growth of the oil rich Niger Delta region. With these arrangements, it is expected that there will be greater understanding and social unrest will reduce in the region to the benefit of all shareholders.

8.5   SOCIAL RESPONSIBILITY AND MEASURING PERFORMANCE

Every organistion has a mission, the purpose for which it has employed competent specialists to manage the enterprise in terms of achievement of the mission using available limited resources. The mission of a business organisation is the production of goods and services to satisfy human wants.

APPENDICES

APPENDIX 1

PROFESSIONAL ETHICS OF THE CHARTERED INSTITUTE OF MARKETING, UK

The need for Professional Standards is like the need for laws in our society. It includes people from various professions and one significant group of professionals are marketers and sales persons. The code of Professional Standards is a general behavioural guide of ethical manners that safeguards the smooth operation of each profession.

The Chartered Institute of Marketing is the Largest, Oldest, Most Accredited and Most Popular Marketing Organisation in the World. Therefore, its Marketing Standards have to be applied worldwide.

Code of Professional Standards

The Code of Marketing Standards is summarised below:

1. Apply Honesty to Customers, Employees and Employers
2. Don't provide or spread false or misleading information
3. Do not injure the business, reputation, interest of any other member of The Institute with unfair or unprofessional practice
4. Be fair and equitable towards other marketing professionals

5. Show integrity and try to add value to the profession of Marketing
6. Demonstrate knowledge of current Marketing Developments and show excellence in their application
7. Treat sensitive information with strict confidence
8. Apply Business in an ethical and professional manner
9. Demonstrate observation and knowledge of other codes of practice.
10. Comply with the governing laws of the relevant country concerned
11. Demonstrate due diligence in using third party endorsement which must have prior approval
12. Do not use any funds derived by CIM, which do not comply with this code, the powers and obligations included in the Constitution and Member Group Guide
13. Do not cause or permit any breach of this code with your knowledge or intension
14. Be updated with the current developments of the Code

The code is supervised by an Ethics Committee and a Disciplinary Committee. Any complaint about the breach of this code from a Member has to be addressed to the Secretary of the Disciplinary Committee: Moorhall, Cookham, Berkshire, SL6 9QH UK. Full details of the case must be provided. The Member who is accused has to be notified by The Secretary of The Disciplinary Committee and provide his or her explanation of the case.

The Royal Charter, By-laws, General Regulations and The Code of Professional Standards can be viewed at www.cim.co.uk/governance

Professional Marketing Standards

- Employers can use the Framework of Professional Marketing Standards in order to assess, define and develop programmes to improve marketing skills within their own teams.

- Marketers and Marketing Professionals can use Professional Marketing Standards in order to follow a framework that overviews the competencies and skills, they need in their career path.

- The Framework of Professional Marketing Standards includes the following Scope and Business Competencies for Support Staff, Practitioners, Managers and Seniors:

RESEARCH AND ANALYSIS

- Understand Markets (Obtain and Analyse information)

STRATEGY AND PLANNING
- Develop Strategy and Marketing Plans (Influence Strategy Formulation and Produce Marketing Plans)

IMPLEMENTATION OF MARKETING PROGRAMMES

1. **Communicate with Stakeholders (Develop and Deliver Effective Communications)**
2. **Manage Products and Services (Develop and Manage Competitive Products and Services)**
3. **Manage and Set Price (Develop and Implement Competitive Pricing Policies)**
4. **Manage Channels (Develop effective Channels to Market and Provide Support to Channel Members)**
5. **Manage Customer Relationships (Maintain and improve customer relationships, Deliver Effective Customer Service)**
   Manage Programmes and Projects (Plan and Prepare Projects, Manage the Implementation of Programmes and Projects)

MEASURE EFFECTIVENESS
- **Monitor and Evaluate the Effectiveness of Marketing (Measure the Effectiveness of Marketing Activities and Explain the Success or Failure of Marketing Activities)**

BRANDS
- **Develop and Manage Brands and Reputation (Create Effective Brands, Manage Brands and Brand Reputation)**

MANAGE PEOPLE
- Manage Marketing Teams (Develop Teams and Individuals to Enhance Marketing Performance, Work with other Functions and Disciplines, Enhance Own Performance, Manage Change)

ETHICS AND SOCIAL RESPONSIBILITY
- Develop and Promote Ethical Practices (Manage Corporate Social Responsibility, Measure Triple Bottom Line Inputs)

You can review the Full Framework of Professional Marketing Standards at www.cim.co.uk

APPENDIX 2

THE INSTITUTE OF CHARTERED ACCOUNTANTS OF NIGERIA

PROFESSIONAL CODE OF CONDUCT AND GUIDE FOR MEMBERS

Approved 2009

TABLE OF CONTENTS

FOREWORD

The Fundamental function of the Accountancy profession is the protection of public interest. The increasing dynamics of the business environment in which Chartered Accountants operate, has made it necessary for the Institute to review the contents of the Professional Code of Conduct currently in existence. The result of the far-reaching review is contained in these rules of professional conduct for members which will continually guide Chartered Accountants in their business and professional relationships.

Generally, a member of a profession owes certain duties to the public at large, including those who retain or employ him; to the profession itself and to all other members of that profession, even though such duties may at times be at variance with his own personal interests.

This Professional Code of Conduct serves as a guide to members of the Institute, and require strict observance as a condition for continuing membership.

The Institute's enabling Act (Institute of Chartered Accountants Act No. 15 of 1965) and these Rules of Professional Conduct have been drawn in such a way that they will assist members in their approach to problems bearing on professional conduct, which they may have to deal with in the performance of their day to day duties whilst the non-observance of these shall result in disciplinary action if that member is found guilty of misconduct.

For this purpose, misconduct is defined to be any act or default likely to bring discredit to a member, the Institute or the accountancy profession. The Council is of the opinion that a high standard of professional conduct is best maintained by complying with these general provisions, which are not exhaustive because it difficult to lay down a written code which would always operate fairly and not leave loopholes for those who are prepared to keep within the letter of the law but care nothing for its spirit, it is also difficult to specify all those circumstances in which a member may be held liable to have committed professional misconduct as defined above.

The Institute through its Council reserves the right to vary from time to time, these Rules of Professional Conduct which set out its ethical requirements in relation to those professional situations which most commonly arise. The Investigating Panel and the Accountants' Disciplinary Tribunal, will demand compliance from members and strictly enforce the maintenance of high standards of professional conduct required of a Chartered Accountant.

An erring member shall be required to answer questions from the Investigating Panel over any complaint and if found referable, would appear before the Disciplinary Tribunal. In keeping with acceptable international practice, the Investigating Panel and the Accountants' Disciplinary Tribunal act in complete independence of Council; have the authority to enforce ethical standards, exercise disciplinary powers, and are entirely free to decide every case coming before them on its merit. The Investigating Panel and The Accountants' Disciplinary Tribunal act impartially, without fear or favour, affection or ill-will, basing their decisions purely on whether or not matters before them have been proved beyond any reasonable doubt as to or not to constitute a misconduct. The freedom of the Investigating Panel and the Disciplinary Tribunal to act impartially is what all members of the Institute must seek to guard jealously.

The fact that misconduct cannot generally be defined, but has to be determined in each individual case by the facts before the panel and the Tribunal, makes it impossible for the Council to lay down mandatory instructions, the mere breach of which would amount to misconduct.

It follows therefore, that these Rules of Professional Conduct are issued by the Institute as a directive and to assist members to conduct themselves in a manner, which the Council considers appropriate to the profession in general and to the members of the Institute in particular. These Rules must, of course, be read in conjunction with the Institute's Act, other Laws or Act in force and binding on the Chartered Accountant. A Chartered Accountant or member Firm shall not apply less stringent standards than those stated in this code of Ethics. Members who are in doubt as to their correct course of action in particular circumstances should obtain further advice through the Registrar/Chief Executive of the Institute.

ACKNOWLEDGEMENTS

This Professional Code of Conduct for members draws extensively from the guidelines of the International Federation of Accountants (IFAC). Their guidelines had to be substantially adapted to meet the peculiarities of our local environment without compromising ethical standards. We are immensely grateful for the permission to use their materials.

Our appreciation also goes to the World Bank for financing the project.

The Institute is appreciative of the contributions and comments of members, the Investigating Panel, and member firms on the initial draft as well as the efforts of the Secretariat staff.

PART ONE

GENERAL APPLICATION OF THE CODE

CHAPTER ONE 1.0.0 INTRODUCTION AND FUNDAMENTAL PRINCIPLES

1.1.0 INTRODUCTION This Code is in four Parts and has twenty-one chapters. Part one defines and explains the Fundamental Principles upon which the Chartered Accountant performs his duties and provides the conceptual framework for applying those principles. The Chartered Accountant is required to apply this conceptual framework in identifying threats to compliance with the Fundamental Principles, evaluating their significance and, if such threats are other than clearly insignificant, to apply safeguards to eliminate them or reduce them to an acceptable level such that compliance with the fundamental principles is not compromised.

Part two deals with and illustrates how the conceptual framework is to be applied by members in Public Practice.

Part three deals with the rules and regulations guiding members in Business and illustrates how the conceptual framework is to be applied by them.

Part four explains the modus operandi of enforcement of the Rules.

1.1.1 Throughout these Rules the term 'member' includes, except where the context otherwise requires, a firm or practice and the term 'partner' includes a director of a body corporate. For the position of affiliates see paragraph 1.1.9 below. To make the language of the Rules simpler and more direct the male pronoun is used throughout to refer to all members regardless of gender; the same technique is employed where possessives are used for the first time and the terms Institute and or ICAN will refer to the Institute of Chartered Accountants of Nigeria.

1.1.2 A distinguishing mark of the accountancy profession is its acceptance of the responsibility to act in the public interest. Therefore, a Chartered Accountant's responsibility is not exclusively to satisfy the needs of an individual client or employer. In acting in the public interest Chartered Accountants should observe and comply with the ethical requirements of this Code.

1.1.3 In addition to the duties owed to the public and to his client or employer, a member of the Institute is bound to observe high standards of Professional conduct. These Rules are to aid members in the identification of occasions in which they might be at risk of failing to recognize or conform to any of those standards.

1.1.4 One of the principal objectives of the ICAN Act is to maintain high standards of professional practice and conduct by all members. The Act renders members liable to disciplinary action, inter alia , if in the course of carrying out their professional duties or otherwise, they commit any act or default likely to bring discredit to members, the

Institute or the profession of accountancy. Believing that a high standard of practice and conduct is best maintained by such general provisions, the Council nonetheless considers it desirable to be more explicit in specific areas, hence these rules.

1.1.5 *Framework for Application of the Code/ Rules* Duties owed by Chartered Accountants, whether in public Practice or not, to the public, require compliance with certain basic ethics described as Fundamental Principles, which constitute professional behaviour. These Fundamental Principles are followed by Statements, which on the other hand are a more elaborate presentation of what is expected from members in certain circumstances.

1.1.6 The Council also herein appropriately defines the practice of accountancy in all its ramifications so that members will be aware of the scope of practice of a Chartered Accountant. The ICAN Act enables the Council of the Institute to widen the scope of the practice of accountancy and its allied subjects.

1.1.7 *Definition of Accountancy* Accountancy Practice includes Assurance, Investigation, Forensic accounting, Tax Practice, Consultancy Practice, Insolvency and Receivership, Financial Advisory Services.

1.1.8 *Students* Students are bound by the ethical requirements of the Institute. They also remain bound during the period between the successful completion of the examinations and their admission to membership, at which point, of course, they become subject to the same requirements in their new capacity.

1.1.9 *Affiliates.* Affiliates, i.e. non-members being in close business connection, allied and associated with a member governed by these Regulations are bound by the Fundamental Principles and, so far as is relevant to practising members, by these Statements.

1.1.10 *Continuity of Practice* Members must ensure that they make arrangement for the continuity in the management of their practice in the case of their death or incapacity. This is particularly important for sole practitioners.

1.1.11 *Sole Practitioner* A sole practitioner that entered into an agreement with another firm for the provision of continuity should find a compatible practice where procedures, fee structure and the work in general are of a similar nature.

Members should ensure that their executors and family are aware, in the event of the member's death or incapacity, of the arrangements made for the management of the practice.

1.1.12 *Failure to Follow the Rules* A member is expected to follow the guidance contained in the fundamental Principles. Failure to follow the rules constitutes an act of professional misconduct or an act of infamous conduct as the case may be. In determining whether or not a complaint is proved, the Accountants' Disciplinary Tribunal may have regard to any code of practice, ethical or technical, and to any regulation affecting members or member firms laid down by the Council.

1.1.13 In considering a complaint of misconduct against a member, the Disciplinary Tribunal may also have regard to any Accounting Guideline and other Regulations of the Council as spelt out in the Rules and Regulations of the Institute.

1.1.14 Enforcement of Ethical Standards The power of the Institute to enforce ethical standards is conferred by the ICAN Act   on the Accountants' Disciplinary Tribunal, which is, in respect of this power, independent of the Council. Details of the enforcement process and procedures are discussed in more details in Part four of this code.

1.2.0. Fundamental Principles A Chartered Accountant is required to comply with the following fundamental principles:

(a) Integrity A Chartered Accountant should be straightforward and honest in all professional and business relationships. Integrity implies not merely honesty but fair dealing and truthfulness.

(b) Objectivity Objectivity is the state of mind, which has regard to all considerations relevant to the task in hand but no other consideration. A Chartered Accountant should not allow bias, conflict of interest or undue influence to override his professional or business judgments.

(c) Professional Competence and Due Care A Chartered Accountant has a continuing duty to maintain professional knowledge and skill at the level required to ensure that a client or employer receives competent professional service based on current developments in practice, legislation and techniques. A member should not accept or perform work, which he is not competent to undertake unless he obtains such advice and assistance as will enable him so to do.

A Chartered Accountant should act diligently and in accordance with applicable technical and professional standards when providing professional services. A member should carry out his professional work with due skill, care, diligence and expedition and with proper regard for the technical and professional standards expected of him as a member.

(d) Confidentiality A Chartered Accountant should respect the confidentiality of information acquired as a result of professional and business relationships and should not disclose any such information to third parties without proper and specific authority unless there is a legal or professional right or duty to disclose. Confidential information acquired as a result of professional and business relationships should not be used for the personal advantage of the Chartered Accountant or third parties.

(e) Professional Behaviour A Chartered Accountant should comply with relevant laws and regulations and should avoid any action that discredits the profession.

A member should conduct himself with courtesy and consideration towards all with whom he comes in contact during the course of performing his work.

Each of these fundamental principles is discussed in detail below:

1.2.1 Integrity   The principle of integrity imposes an obligation on all Chartered Accountants to be straightforward and honest in professional and business relationships. Integrity also implies fair dealing and truthfulness.

A Chartered Accountant should not be associated with reports, returns, communications or other information where they believe that the information:

(a) Contains a materially false or misleading statement:

(b) Contains statements or information furnished recklessly: or (c) Omits or obscures information required to be included where such omission or obscurity would be misleading.

A member's advice and work must be uncorrupted by self-interest and not be unduly influenced by the interests of other parties.

1.2.2 Objectivity

(a) The principle of objectivity imposes an obligation on Chartered Accountants to be fair, intellectually honest and free of conflicts of interest. Regardless of service or capacity, Chartered Accountants should protect the integrity of their professional services, and maintain objectivity in their judgment.

(b) In selecting the situations and practices to be specifically dealt with in ethics requirements relating to objectivity, adequate consideration should be given to the following factors:-

(i) Chartered Accountants are exposed to situations, which involve the possibility of pressures being exerted on them. These pressures may impair their objectivity.

(ii) Relationships should be avoided which allow prejudice, bias or influences of others to override objectivity.

(iii) Chartered Accountants have an obligation to ensure that personnel engaged on professional services adhere to the principle of objectivity.

(iv) Chartered Accountants should neither accept nor offer gifts or entertainment, which might reasonably be believed to have a significant and improper influence on their professional judgment or those with whom they deal. What constitutes an excessive gift or offer of entertainment varies from situation to situation but Chartered Accountants should avoid circumstances, which would bring their professional standing into disrepute.

1.2.3. Professional Competence and Due Care (a) The principle of professional competence and due care imposes the following obligations on Chartered Accountants:

(i) To maintain professional knowledge and skill at the level required to ensure that clients or employers receive competent professional service; and

(ii) To act diligently in accordance with applicable technical and professional standards when providing professional services.

(b) Competent professional service requires the exercise of sound judgment in applying professional knowledge and skill in the performance of such service. Professional competence may be divided into two separate phases:

(i) Attainment of professional competence (certification); and

(ii) Maintenance of professional competence (Continuing Education).

(c) The maintenance of professional competence requires a continuing awareness and an understanding of relevant technical professional and business developments. Continuing professional development e.g. Members Continuing Professional Education (MCPE) develops and maintains the capabilities that enable a Chartered Accountant to continue performing competently within the professional environment.

(d) Diligence encompasses the responsibility to act in accordance with the requirements of an assignment, carefully, thoroughly and on a timely basis.

(e) A Chartered Accountant should take steps to ensure that those working under his authority in a professional capacity have appropriate training and supervision. Where appropriate, a Chartered Accountant shall make clients, employers or other users of his professional services aware of limitations inherent in the services to avoid the misinterpretation of an expression of opinion as an assertion of fact.

1.2.4. Confidentiality (a) The principle of confidentiality imposes an obligation on Chartered Accountants to refrain from:

(i) Disclosing to persons outside the firm and on a need to know basis to persons within the firm or employing organization, confidential information acquired as a result of professional and business relationships without proper and specific authority unless there is a legal or professional right or duty to disclose such; and,

(ii) Using confidential information acquired as a result of professional and business relationships to their personal advantage or the advantage of third parties.

(b) Chartered Accountants should maintain confidentiality even in a social environment.

(c) Chartered Accountants should be alert to the possibility of inadvertent disclosure, particularly in circumstances involving long association with a business associate or a close or immediate family member.

(d) Chartered Accountants should also maintain confidentiality of information disclosed by a prospective client or employer.

(e) Chartered Accountants should consider the need to maintain confidentiality of information within the firm or employing organisation.

(f) Chartered Accountants should take all reasonable steps to ensure that staff under his control and persons from whom advice and assistance is obtained respect the Chartered Accountant's duty of confidentiality.

(g) The need to comply with the principle of confidentiality continues even after the end of relationships between a Chartered Accountant and a client or employer when a Chartered Accountant changes employment or acquires a new client as, he is entitled to use prior experience. The Chartered Accountant should not, however, use or disclose any confidential information either acquired or received as a result of a professional or business relationship.

(h) The following are circumstances where Chartered Accountants are or may be required to disclose confidential information or when such disclosure may be appropriate:

(i) Disclosure is permitted by law and or is authorised by the client or the employer;

(ii) Disclosure is required by law, for example:

(a) Production of documents or other provision of evidence in the course of legal proceedings; or

(b) Disclosure to the appropriate public authorities of infringements of the law that came to light; and

(iii) There is a professional duty or right to disclose, when not prohibited by law:

(a) To comply with the quality review of a member body or professional body;

13

(b) To respond to an inquiry or investigation by a member body or regulatory body;

(c) To protect the professional interests of a Chartered Accountant in legal proceedings; or

(d)   To comply with technical standards and ethics requirements.

(e) Other similar situations not covered by (a) to (d) above

(i) In deciding whether or not to disclose confidential information, Chartered Accountants should consider the following points:

(a) Whether the interests of all parties, including third parties whose interests may be affected, could be harmed if the client or employer consents to the disclosure of information by the Chartered Accountant;

(b) Whether all the relevant information is known and substantiated, to the extent that it is practicable; when the situation involves unsubstantiated facts, incomplete information or unsubstantiated conclusions, professional judgment should be used in determining the type of disclosure to be made, if any; and

(d) The type of communication that is expected and to whom it is addressed; in particular, Chartered Accountants should be satisfied that the parties to whom the communication is addressed are appropriate recipients.

1.2.5. Professional Behaviour

(a) The principle of professional behaviour imposes an obligation on Chartered Accountants to comply with relevant laws and regulations and avoid any action that may bring discredit to the profession. This includes actions which would make a reasonably informed third party conclude negatively about the good reputation of the profession.

(b) In marketing and promoting themselves and their work, Chartered Accountants   should not bring the profession into disrepute. Chartered Accountants should be honest and truthful and should not:

(i) Make exaggerated claims of the services they are able to offer, the qualifications they possess, or experience they have gained; or

(ii) Make disparaging references or unsubstantiated comparisons to the work of others.

CHAPTER TWO

2.1.0 CONCEPTUAL FRAMEWORK GUIDING COMPLIANCE WITH THE FUNDAMENTAL PRINCIPLES.

2.1.1 CONCEPTUAL FRAMEWORK It is difficult to define every situation that creates threats to compliance with the Fundamental Principles and specify the appropriate mitigating actions. The nature of engagements and work assignments of the Chartered Accountant differs and consequently the threats to same may differ, thus requiring the application of different safeguards.

2.1.2 It is therefore reasonable to provide a conceptual framework within which a Chartered Accountant should operate in identifying, evaluating and addressing threats to compliance with the fundamental principles rather than merely complying with a set of specific rules, which may be arbitrary. This Code attempts to provide such a framework.

2.1.3 While the Chartered Accountant has an obligation to evaluate any threats to compliance with the fundamental principles, he is also expected to take qualitative as well as quantitative factors into account when considering the significance of a threat. Where a Chartered Accountant cannot implement appropriate safeguards, he should decline or discontinue the specific professional service involved, or where necessary, resign from the client (in the case of a Chartered Accountant in public practice) or the employing organization (in the case of a Chartered Accountant in business).

2.1.4 The examples given in this code are intended to illustrate how the conceptual framework is to be applied. The examples are not intended to be, nor should they be interpreted as, an exhaustive list of all circumstances experienced by a Chartered Accountant that may create threats to compliance with the fundamental principles. Consequently, it is not sufficient for the Chartered Accountant merely to comply with the examples presented; rather, the framework should be applied to the particular circumstances encountered by the Chartered Accountant.

2.0 THREATS AND SAFEGUARDS:

2.2.0 THREATS TO COMPLIANCE WITH THE FUNDAMENTAL PRINCIPLES

Compliance with the fundamental Principles may potentially be threatened by a broad range of circumstances, which fall into the following categories,

(a) Self-interest threats, which may occur as a result of the financial or other interests of a Chartered Accountant or of an immediate or close family member;

(b) Self review threats, which may occur when a previous judgment needs to be re- evaluated by the Chartered Accountant responsible for that judgment;

(c) Advocacy threats, which may occur when a Chartered Accountant promotes a position or opinion to the point that subsequent objectivity may be compromised;

(d) Familiarity threats, which may occur when, a Chartered Accountant becomes too sympathetic to the interests of others because of a close relationship (e) Intimidation threats, which may occur when a Chartered Accountant may be deterred from acting objectively by threats, actual or perceived.

2.2.1 SAFEGUARDS Safeguards are intended to eliminate or reduce threats to an acceptable level, and they fall into two broad categories:

(a) Safeguards created by the profession, legislation or regulation; (b) Safeguards within the assurance client; and within the firm's own systems and procedures.

Chartered Accountants should select appropriate safeguards to eliminate or reduce threats to the fundamental principles to an acceptable level, other than those threats that are clearly insignificant. Parts two and three of this code respectively, discuss

Safeguards in the work environment for Chartered Accountants in Public Practice and those in Business.

2.3.0 Ethical Conflict Resolution In evaluating compliance with the fundamental principles, a Chartered Accountant may be required to resolve a conflict in the application of fundamental principles.

2.3.1 When initiating either a formal or informal conflict resolution process, a Chartered Accountant should consider the following, either individually or together with others, as part of the resolution process: (a) Relevant facts; (b) Ethical issues involved; (c) Fundamental principles related to the matter in question; (d) Established internal procedures; and (e) Alternative courses of action.

2.3.2 Having considered these issues, a Chartered Accountant should determine the appropriate course of action that is consistent with the fundamental principles identified. The Chartered Accountant should also weigh the consequences of each possible course of action. If the matter remains unresolved, he should consult with other appropriate persons within the firm or employing organization for help in obtaining resolution.

2.3.3 Where a matter involves a conflict with, or within, an organization, a Chartered Accountant should also consider consulting with those charged with governance of the organization, such as the board of directors or the audit committee.

2.3.4 It may be in the best interest of the Chartered Accountant to document the substance of the issue and details of any discussions held or decisions taken, concerning that issue.

2.3.5 If a significant conflict cannot be resolved, a Chartered Accountant may wish to obtain professional advice from the relevant Faculty of the Institute or legal advisors, and thereby obtain guidance on ethical issues without breaching confidentiality. For example, a Chartered Accountant may have encountered a fraud, the reporting of which could breach the Chartered Accountant's responsibility to respect confidentiality. The Chartered Accountant should consider obtaining legal advice to determine whether or not there is a requirement to report.

2.3.6 If, after exhausting all relevant possibilities, the ethical conflict remains unresolved, a Chartered Accountant should, where possible, refuse to remain associated with the matter creating the conflict. The Chartered Accountant may determine that, in the circumstances, it is appropriate to withdraw from the engagement team, or specific assignment, or to resign altogether from the engagement, the firm or the employing organization.

PART TWO

CHARTERED ACCOUNTANTS IN PUBLIC PRACTICE
CHAPTER THREE

     3.0 INTRODUCTION   This Part of the Code illustrates how the conceptual framework contained in Part One is to be applied by Chartered Accountants in public practice. The examples in the following Chapters are not intended to be, nor should they be interpreted as, an exhaustive list of all circumstances experienced by Chartered Accountants in public practice that may create threats to compliance with the principles. Consequently, it is not sufficient for a Chartered Accountant in public practice merely to comply with the examples presented; rather, the framework should be applied to the particular circumstances faced.

     3.1.1 A Chartered Accountant in public practice should not engage in any business, occupation or activity that impairs or might impair integrity, objectivity or the good reputation of the profession and as a result would be incompatible with the rendering of professional services.

     3.2.0 Threats and Safeguards:

     Threats: Compliance with the fundamental principles may potentially be threatened by a broad range of circumstances, which may fall into the following categories: (a)   Self Interest (b)   Self Review (c)   Advocacy (d)   Familiarity (e)   Intimidation

     3.2.1 Threats can arise in a number of ways, some are general in nature and some are related to the specific circumstances of an assignment or role. Members should identify the threats and consider them in the light of the environment in which they are working. They should also take into account the safeguards, which assist them to withstand threats and risks to the fundamental Principles.

     3.2.2 Categories of threats   (a) The Self-interest threat: This is a threat to the auditor's objectivity stemming from a financial or other self-interest conflict. This could arise, from a fear of losing a client. Examples of circumstances that may create self-interest threats for Chartered Accountants in public practice include, but are not limited to:

     (i)   A financial interest in a client or jointly holding a financial interest with a client.

     (ii)   Undue dependence on total fees from a client, and an unduly large proportion will normally be 25% and above which is inclusive of repetitive one-off assignments.

     (iii) Having a close business relationship with a client.
     (iv) Concern about the possibility of losing a client.
     (v) Potential employment with a client.
     (vi) Contingent fees relating to an assurance engagement.
     (vii) A loan to or from an assurance client or any of its directors or officers.
     (b) The self review threat This occurs when:

(i) any product or judgment of a previous assurance engagement or non-assurance engagement needs to be re-evaluated in reaching conclusions on the assurance engagement or

(ii) when a member of the assurance team was previously a director or officer of the assurance client, or was an employee in a position to exert direct and significant influence over the subject matter of the assurance engagement. This threat is even more pronounced in the small and medium sized firms. Examples of circumstances that may create self-review threats include, but are not limited to.

(a) The discovery of a significant error during a re-evaluation of the work of the Chartered Accountant in public practice.

(b) Reporting on the operation of financial systems after being involved in their design or implementation. This is very common in our environment and therefore firms should take special care to look out for such threats.

(c) Having prepared the original data used to generate records that are the subject matter of the engagement. This is also in the same category with (ii) above.

(d) A member of the assurance team being, or having recently been, a director or officer of that client.

(e) A member of the assurance team being, or having recently been, employed by the client in a position to exert direct and significant influence over the subject matter of the engagement.

(f) Performing a service for a client that directly affects the subject matter of the assurance engagement.

(c) The Advocacy threat; There is an apparent threat to the auditor's objectivity, if he becomes an advocate for (or against) his client's position in any adversarial proceeding or situation. Whenever the auditor takes a strongly proactive stance on the client's behalf, this may appear to be incompatible with the special objectivity that audit requires. Examples of circumstances that may create advocacy threats include, but are not limited to:

(i) Promoting shares in a quoted entity when that entity is a financial statement audit client.

(ii) Acting as an advocate on behalf of an assurance client in litigation or disputes with third parties.

(iii) Acting as a reporting accountant in an entity when that entity is a financial statement audit client.

(d) The familiarity or trust threat: A threat where the auditor, by virtue of a close relationship with an assurance client, its directors, officers or employees, a firm or a member of the assurance team becomes too sympathetic to the client's interests. Examples of circumstances that may create familiarity threats include, but are not limited to:

(i) A member of the engagement team having a close or immediate Family relationship with a director or officer of the client.

(ii) A member of the engagement team having a close or immediate family relationship with an employee of the client who is in a position to exert direct and significant influence over the subject matter of the engagement.

(iii)   A former partner of the firm being a director or officer of the client or an employee in a position to exert direct and significant influence over the subject matter of the engagement.

(iv) Accepting gifts or preferential treatment from a client, unless the value is clearly insignificant (the reasonable man's judgment will be the yardstick for insignificance.)

(v)   Long association of senior personnel with the assurance client.

(e) Intimidation threat: occurs when a member of the assurance team may be deterred from acting objectively and exercising professional skepticism by threats, actual or perceived, from the directors, officers or employees of an assurance client.

Examples of circumstances that may create intimidation threats include, but are not limited to:

i) Being threatened with dismissal or replacement in relation to a client engagement.

ii) Being threatened with litigation.

iii) Being pressured to reduce inappropriately the extent of work performed in order to reduce fees.

3.2.3 The list above is not exhaustive; consequently members should take cognizance of other situations that may pose threats not considered above.

3.2.4 The firm and members of the assurance team have a responsibility to remain independent by taking into account the context in which they practice, the threats to independence and the safeguards available to eliminate the threats or reduce them to an acceptable level.

3.2.5 When threats are identified, other than those that are clearly insignificant, appropriate safeguards should be identified and applied to eliminate the threats or reduce them to an acceptable level. This decision should be documented. (It should be part of the working paper file).

3.2.6 In accepting an assignment all Chartered Accountants must carry out a risk assessment. The assessment must include, but should not be limited to, a review of the industry, the nature of the business and the management team.

3.2.7 SAFEGUARDS AND PROCEDURES Safeguards fall into two broad categories:

(a) Safeguards created by the profession, legislation or regulation;

(b) Safeguards within the work environment (That is, at the assurance clients' and within the firm's own systems and procedures).

The firm and the members of the assurance team should select appropriate safeguards to eliminate or reduce threats to independence, other than those that are clearly insignificant, to an acceptable level.

3.2.8 Safeguards created by the profession, legislation or regulation, include the following but are not restricted to:

(a)   Educational, training and experience requirements for entry into the profession;

(b) Continuing Professional Development requirements;

(c) Professional standards and monitoring and disciplinary processes;

(d) External review of a firm's quality control system by a legally empowered third party of the reports, returns, communications or information produced by a Chartered Accountant; e.g. peer review, regulatory professional review etc.

(e) Legislation governing the independence requirements of the firm. e.g. Companies and Allied Matters Act.

(f) Corporate governance regulations.

3.2.9 Safeguards within the work environment include the following:

(a) When the assurance client's management appoints the firm, persons other than management ratify or approve the appointment;

(b) The assurance client has competent employees to take managerial decisions;

(c) Policies and procedures that emphasize the assurance client's commitment to fair financial reporting;

(d) Internal procedures that ensure objective choices in commissioning non assurance engagements; and

(f) A corporate governance structure, such as an audit committee, peer review that provide appropriate oversight function regarding a firm's services.

3.2.10 Safeguards are also:

(a) The long standing rules of professional conduct for members of which this guidance forms part. Where appropriate, these rules impose specific prohibitions where the threats to the auditors' objectivity is so significant or is generally perceived to be so, that no other appropriate safeguards will be effective.

(b) The ethical support provided by the Institute e.g the investigating Panel and the Disciplinary Tribunal.

(c) The reinforcement given to the above safeguards by the policing system which reacts to complaints whether by members of the public or members of the profession, investigates the background to the complaints and when necessary commence disciplinary proceedings against an offending member. Together with monitoring procedures below, the system ensures that the firm's past conduct and current procedures are likely to come under close independent professional scrutiny, if the conduct of practising members give rise to challenges over the exercise of these roles.

(d) The active monitoring procedures conducted by the profession constitute a form of safeguard. On behalf of the Institute, the Professional Practice Monitoring Committee (PPMC) may visit firms which conduct audit and examine compliance with audit guidelines and sound professional practice.

3.2.11 Auditors should always use the above safeguards, i.e. profession, legislation or regulation, safeguards of the assurance client or the firm's own systems and procedures to reduce threats.

3.2.12 Certain safeguards may increase the likelihood of identifying or deterring unethical behaviour. Such safeguards, which may be created by the accounting profession, legislation, regulation or an employing organization, include, but are not restricted to:

(a) Effective, well publicized complaints systems operated by the employing organization, the profession or a regulator, which enable colleagues, employers and members of the public, draw attention to unprofessional or unethical behaviour.

(b) An explicitly stated duty to report breaches of ethical requirements.

3.2.13. The nature of the safeguards to be applied will vary depending on the circumstances. In exercising professional judgment, a Chartered Accountant should consider what a reasonable and informed third party, having knowledge of all relevant information, including the significance of the threat and the safeguards applied, would conclude to be unacceptable.

EXAMPLES OF SOME THREATS AND SAFEGUARDS

3.3.0.   SELF INTEREST THREATS.

3.3.1   AREA OF RISK   *Undue dependence on an Audit Client. See paragraphs 3.2.2. (a) ii. For further examples see paragraphs 16.1.1*

3.3.2 SAFEGUARDS   *It is the responsibility of both the audit engagement partner and the management of the firm to ensure that in such a situation, additional safeguards are introduced by way of second partner review and support to ensure that objectivity of judgment is retained by the partner responsible for engagement decisions and audit judgments. For further information, see paragraph 16.1.2.*

3.3.3   AREA OF RISK   *Principal or senior employee joining client, threatens the Firm's objectivity thereby creating a self interest threat. For further information, see paragraph 16.1. 10 .*

3.3.4   SAFEGUARDS   *For further information see paragraph 16.1. 11.*   3.3.5 *AREA OF RISK mutual business interest. A mutual business interest with a client company or with an officer or employee of the company will create a self –interest threat.*

3.3.6   SAFEGUARDS   *Where such an interest exists, the engagement should not be accepted.*

3.3.7   AREA OF RISK *beneficial interests in shares and other investments. A beneficial interest is a beneficial shareholding or other direct investment in the company. Beneficial interest on the part of a principal or anyone closely connected with a principal of the audit firm in a client company will constitute an insurmountable self-interest threat. (See further explanations in paragraphs 16.1.12.*

3.3.8   SAFEGUARDS   *Where an employee, or a person closely connected with an employee, has such a beneficial interest, the employee should not take part in the audit of the client company.*

(a) Beneficial shareholding is not intended to preclude a principal or a person closely connected with a principal from holding or continuing to hold, in the   normal course of business and on normal commercial terms, an insurance or   pension policy with a client insurance company or society, though an engagement partner should not take out a new policy with such a client.

(b) A beneficial holding in an authorized unit or investment trust, which holds shares in a client company is also not precluded.

3.3.9   AREA OF RISK *Loans to or from a client, guarantee, overdue fees. etc*

3.3.10 SAFEGUARD A Chartered Accountant should not take a loan from a client. See Banks and other Financial Institutions Act and paragraph 16.1.3

3.3.11 Areas of Risk Participation in the affairs of clients is likely to lead to self interest or familiarity threat

3.3.12 SAFEGUARD The Chartered Accountant shall not take up such an appointment. For further information, see paragraph 16.1.8

3.3.13 AREA OF RISK Beneficial interests in trusts.

A beneficial interest in a trust is a beneficiary in a trust or foundation, which include a trustee of such a trust or foundation. Any beneficial interest by the auditor or principal of the assurance firm in the trust, constitutes an insurmountable self interest threat.

3.3.14 SAFEGUARDS (i) A beneficial interest in a trust having a shareholding in an audit client company (i.e. a Foundation or Trust) should be regarded as a beneficial interest in the Client's Company and therefore shall not take part in the audit of that client.

(ii) Where the principal or a person closely connected with him holds the beneficial interest in a trust, and where the principal is not a trustee, he should cease personally to take part in the audit of the company as soon as he becomes aware of the shareholding.

3.3.15 COMMENTS (a) Paragraph 3.3.7 above is not intended to preclude a principal or a person closely connected with a principal from holding or continuing to hold, in the normal course of business and on normal commercial terms, an insurance or pension policy with a client insurance company or society, though an engagement partner should not take out a new policy with such a client, nor is a beneficial holding in an authorized unit or investment trust which holds shares in a client company so precluded.

(b) Principal in an audit firm may invest in unit trusts or in an investment trust, provided that the firm does not report upon the trust.

Where a principal inherits shares or marries a shareholder, or a relevant investment occurs as a result of a takeover, the investment should be disposed off at the earliest practicable date, being a date at which the transaction would not amount to insider dealing. Similar action should be taken where a beneficial investment is held in a company becoming an audit client. Where the necessary disposal cannot be achieved within the time scale envisaged, the firm should not continue as auditor.

3.4.0 SELF REVIEW THREAT. Examples of circumstances that may create self-review threats include, but are not limited to:

3.4.1 AREA OF RISK

(a) The discovery of a significant error during a re-evaluation of the work of the Chartered Accountant in public practice.

(b) Reporting on the operation of financial systems after being involved in their design or implementation.

3.4.2 SAFEGUARD Every Chartered Accountant in practice should be aware of this threat. This is particularly important in the case of a sole practitioner. Where practicable the sole practitioner should explore the possibility of peer review for such assurance clients. In the case of big firms, engagement partners should be rotated every four years.

>   3.4.3   AREA OF RISK

Having prepared the original data used to generate records that are the subject matter of the engagement.

>   3.4.4 SAFEGUARD The audit team that designed the system or generated the records should not be involved in the assurance function. A sole Practitioner shall not audit a system, the design of which he undertook.

>   3.4.5   AREA OF RISK A member of the assurance team being, or having recently been, a director or officer of that client.   3.4.6 SAFEGUARD   That officer should be excluded from the assurance team.

>   3.4.7   AREA OF RISK

A member of the assurance team being, or having recently been, employed by the client in a position to exert direct and significant influence over the subject matter of the engagement.

>   3.4.8   SAFEGUARD In circumstances where a member of the Assurance team becomes an employee of an assurance client, the safeguard will be that somebody that could resist influences of the new assurance client's employee must lead the Assurance team. Specifically, if an assurance client engages an audit manager, the Assurance team should be led by his equivalent or above in the firm.

>   3.4.9 AREA OF RISK   Performing a service e.g Consultancy Services, for a client that directly affects the   subject matter of the assurance engagement.

>   3.4.10   SAFEGUARD   The minimum safeguard should be that the person performing that service shall be excluded from the Assurance function. In the case of a sole practitioner, the Firm should choose between the Assurance function or the service.

>   3.5.0 ADVOCACY THREAT

Examples of circumstances that may create advocacy threats include, but are not limited to:

>   3.5.1   AREA OF RISK   Promoting shares in a quoted entity when that entity is a financial statement audit   client.

>   3.5.2   SAFEGUARD The Chartered Accountant in public practice is prohibited from such advocacy or he should resign the engagement.

>   3.5.3   AREA OF RISK   Acting as an advocate on behalf of an assurance client in litigation or disputes with third parties.

>   3.5.4. SAFEGUARD The Chartered Accountant in public Practice is prohibited from such advocacy.

>   3.6.0   FAMILIARITY THREAT   Examples of circumstances that may create familiarity threats include, but are not limited to:

>   3.6.1   AREA OF RISK

A member of the engagement team having a close or immediate family relationship with a director or officer of the client.

3.6.2 SAFEGUARD. Exclude the team member concerned for the audit team.

3.6.3 AREA OF RISK A member of the engagement team having a close or immediate family relationship with an employee of the client who is in a position to exert direct and significant influence over the subject matter of the engagement.

3.6.4. SAFEGUARD Exclude the team member concerned from the audit.

3.6.5 AREA OF RISK A former partner of the firm being a director or officer of the client or an employee in a position to exert direct and significant influence over the subject matter of the engagement.

3.6.6 SAFEGUARD The audit team leader should be of commensurate status to resist such influences.

3.6.7 AREA OF RISK Accepting gifts or preferential treatment from a client, unless the value is clearly insignificant.

3.6.8 SAFEGUARD If the threat is significant, refuse it.

3.6. 9 AREA OF RISK Long association of senior personnel with the assurance client. 3.6.10 SAFEGUARD Ensure that no audit engagement partner remain in charge of an audit for a period exceeding 5 consecutive years. An audit engagement partner who has ceased to act under this provision should not return to that role till a period of 4 (5)?1 years has elapsed but it is not precluded from other involvement with the client.

3.7.0 INTIMIDATION THREAT Examples of circumstances that may create intimidation threats include, but are not limited to:

3.7.1 AREA OF RISK Being threatened with dismissal or replacement in relation to a client engagement.

3.7.2 SAFEGUARD Ensure that the current audit file complies with all professional standards, guidelines and the relevant laws.

3.7.3 AREA OF RISK Being threatened with litigation. For further information see paragraph 16.1.6

3.7.4 SAFEGUARD (i) Have transparent and up to date standards, guidelines and comply with the relevant laws.

(ii) Seek for legal advise or opinion on such specific areas of disagreement with the client.

3.7.5 AREA OF RISK Being pressured to reduce inappropriately the extent of work performed in order to reduce fees.

3.7.6 SAFEGUARD (i) In negotiating fees, it should not be tied specifically to turnover. The emphasis should be the extent of work and the required levels of skills and manpower, time and charge outrates as recommended by the Institute. If therefore, there is a decline in turn over one can then rely on the basis of one's fee above to defend the sustenance of the fee levels.

(ii) Where the client insists on the reduction of work, prior to the commencement of the assurance function, one should consider disengagement. If however the work has commenced, and the client then insists on the reduction of work, one should consider the qualification of the assurance opinion.

1 To confirm no 3.6.10 line 3 from Committee.

3.8.0 OTHER EXAMPLES. A Chartered Accountant in public practice may also find that specific circumstances give rise to unique threats to compliance with one or more of the fundamental principles. Such unique threats obviously cannot be categorized. In either professional or business relationships, a Chartered Accountant in public practice should always be on the alert for such circumstances and threats.

3.8.1 Examples of safeguards created by the profession, legislation or regulation are described in Chapter 16 of this Code.

In the work environment, the relevant safeguards will vary depending on the circumstances. Work environment safeguards comprise firm-wide safeguards and engagement specific safeguards. A Chartered Accountant in public practice should exercise judgment to determine how to best deal with an identified threat. In exercising this judgment a Chartered Accountant in public practice should consider what a reasonable and informed third party, having knowledge of all relevant information, including the significance of the threat and the safeguards applied, would reasonably conclude to be acceptable. This consideration will be affected by matters such as the significance of the threat, the nature of the engagement and the structure of the firm.

3.8.2 Firm-wide safeguards in the work environment may include:

(a) Leadership of the firm that stresses the importance of compliance with the fundamental principles.

(b) Leadership of the firm that establishes guidelines for accepting new clients and the expectation that members of assurance team will act in the public interest.

(c) Policies and procedures to implement and monitor quality control of engagements.

(d) Documented policies regarding the identification of threats to compliance with the fundamental principles, the evaluation of the significance of these threats, the identification and the application of safeguards to eliminate or reduce the threats, other than those that are clearly insignificant, to an acceptable level.

(e) For firms that perform assurance engagements, documented independence policies regarding the identification of threats to independence, the evaluation of the significance of these threats and the application of safeguards to eliminate or reduce the threats, other than those that are clearly insignificant, to an acceptable level.

(i) Documented internal policies and procedures requiring compliance with the fundamental principles.

(ii) Policies and procedures that will enable the identification of interests or relationships between the firm or members of engagement teams and clients.

(iii) Policies and procedures to monitor and, if necessary, manage the reliance of revenue received from a single client.

(iv) Using different partners and engagement teams with separate reporting lines for the provision of non-assurance services to an assurance client.

(v) Policies and procedures to prohibit individuals who are not members of an engagement team from inappropriately influencing the outcome of the engagement.

(vi) Timely communication of a firm's policies and procedures, including any changes to these policies and procedures, to all partners and professional staff, and appropriate training and education on such policies and procedures.

(vii) Designating a member of senior management to be responsible for overseeing the adequate functioning of the firm's quality control system.

(viii) Advising partners and professional staff of those assurance clients and related entities from which they must be independent.

(ix) A disciplinary mechanism to promote compliance with policies and procedures.

(x) Published policies and procedures to encourage and empower staff to communicate to senior levels within the firm any issue relating to compliance with the fundamental principles that concerns them.

In implementing all of the above, a Chartered Accountant should use a checklist, which must be reviewed at regular intervals of every two years.

3.8.3 Engagement-specific safeguards in the work environment may include:

(a) Involving an additional Chartered Accountant to review the work done or otherwise advise as necessary.

(b) Consulting an independent third party, such as a committee of independent directors, a professional regulatory body or another Chartered Accountant.

(c) Discussing ethical issues with those charged with governance of the client.

(d) Disclosing to those charged with governance of the client the nature of services provided and extent of fees charged.

(e) Rotating senior assurance team personnel.

3.8.4 Depending on the nature of the engagement, a Chartered Accountant in public practice may also be able to rely on safeguards that the client has implemented after review and acceptance. However it is not advisable to rely solely on such safeguards to reduce threats to an acceptable level.

3.8.5 Safeguards within the client's systems and procedures may include when:

(a) A client appoints a firm in public practice to perform an engagement, persons other than management ratify or approve the appointment.

(b) The client has competent employees with experience and seniority to make managerial decisions.

(c) The client has implemented internal procedures that ensure objective choices in commissioning non-assurance engagements.

(d) The client has a corporate governance structure that provides appropriate oversight and communications regarding the firm's services.

3.9.0 Review Procedures for Safeguards: These are steps taken by firms to ensure that threats to objectivity are recognized, documented and mitigated.

a) Wherever review procedures indicate that an audit assignment should be accepted or continued only with additional safeguards against loss of objectivity, the engagement partner's decision and the range of safeguards appropriate to the assignment should be subject to independent review by a partner not connected with the engagement.

b) The Safeguards to be applied should include, as appropriate, rotation of the audit engagement partner and of senior audit staff. In particular the firm should review annually the possible need for the rotation of an audit engagement partner.

c) A record of all safeguards applied during the review process should be kept.

d) To the extent that a small firm may find difficultly in implementing the safeguards, principals should set up external consultation arrangements appropriate to their particular circumstances

e) Where the practitioner's own review indicates that an audit engagement should only be accepted or continued with additional safeguards to protect his independence, he should undertake such consultation as stated in (d) above before proceeding further. The extent of the consultation will vary according to the nature of the problem. In some cases it may be confined to a discussion of principles; in others it may involve an examination of the file or a discussion of personal relationships.

f) A sole practitioner should not accept or continue appointment as auditor of a company at a time when he is a trustee of a trust holding shares in that company.

3.10.0 Guidance on some Threats and Safeguards

3.10.1 Undue dependence on an Audit Client:

If the recurring fees from a client company or group of companies constitute a substantial proportion of the fee income of an audit firm, a self-interest threat is likely to arise so as to impair objectivity. Detailed discussion on this possible threat is given in paragraphs16.1.2 to −16.1.3 (a– e).

3.10.2. Audit committees can have an important corporate governance role when they are knowledgeable in audit practices and are independent of client management. There should be regular communication between the firm and the audit committee.

3.10.3. Firms should establish policies and procedures relating to independent communications with audit committees, or others charged with governance. Safeguards within the firm's own systems and procedures may include firm wide safeguards such as the following:

(a) Firm leadership that stresses the importance of independence and the expectation that members of assurance teams will act in the public interest;

(b) Policies and procedures to implement and monitor quality control of assurance engagements;

(c) Documented independence policies regarding the identification of threats to independence, the evaluation of the significance of these threats and the identification and application of safeguards to eliminate or reduce the threats, other than those that are clearly insignificant, to an acceptable level;

(d) Internal policies and procedures to monitor compliance with firm policies and procedures as they relate to independence;

(e) Policies and procedures that will enable the identification of interests or relationships between the firm or members of the assurance team and assurance clients;

(f) Policies and procedures to monitor and, if necessary, manage the reliance on revenue received from a single assurance client;

(g) Using different partners and teams with separate reporting lines for the provision of non-assurance services to an assurance client;

(h) Policies and procedures to prohibit individuals who are not members of the assurance team from influencing the outcome of the assurance engagement;

(i) Timely communication of a firm's policies and procedures, and any changes thereto, to all partners and professional staff, including appropriate training and education thereon;

(j) Designating a member of senior management as responsible for overseeing the adequate functioning of the safeguarding system;

(k) Means of advising partners and professional staff of those assurance clients and related entities from which they must be independent;

(l) A disciplinary mechanism to promote compliance with policies and procedures; and

(m) Policies and procedures to empower staff to communicate to senior levels within the firm any issue of independence and objectivity that concerns them; this includes informing staff of the procedures open to them.

3.11.0. Safeguarding Objectivity   In order to safeguard their objectivity, members should consider certain matters before deciding whether or not to accept any appointment. The matters to be considered include those under the following headings:

(a) The expectations of those directly affected or likely to be affected by the work.

(b) The public interest and its bearing on the work.

(c) The threat to objectivity, which may arise actually or potentially.

(d) The safeguards which are or can be put in place, overt or otherwise, to offset the threats.

3.11.1   The responsibility for seeing that the above matters are properly considered   resides ultimately, in the case of members in practice, with the engagement partner who takes the primary responsibility for the client concerned. Firms should establish reliable procedures to ensure that the matters are properly addressed. These may include but not limited to:

(a) The expectations of those directly affected (or likely to be affected by the work) are likely to be concerned about the existence of any relationship or situation affecting a member or firm, or any business or other interest held by the member or firm, which may threaten or appear to threaten objectivity. Accordingly, the member concerned must disclose the relationship, situation or interest to the affected parties.

(b) The Public Interest should be a factor, which all members should bear in mind when accepting any assignment or appointment.

CHAPTER FOUR
4.1.0 PROFESSIONAL APPOINTMENTS.
    4.1.1 Client Acceptance.
    Before accepting a new client relationship, a Chartered Accountant in public practice should consider whether acceptance would create any threats to compliance with the fundamental principles. Potential threats to integrity or professional behaviour may be created from, for example, questionable issues associated with the client (its owners, management and activities).
    4.1.2   Client issues that, if known, could threaten compliance with the fundamental principles include, for example, client involvement in illegal activities (such as money laundering), dishonesty or questionable financial reporting practices.
    4.1.3 The significance of any threats should be evaluated. If identified threats are other than clearly insignificant, safeguards should be considered and applied as necessary to eliminate or reduce them to an acceptable level.
    4.1.4   Appropriate safeguards may include obtaining knowledge and understanding of the client, its owners, managers and those responsible for its governance and business activities, or securing the client's commitment to improve corporate governance practices or internal controls.
    4.1.5 Where it is not possible to reduce the threats to an acceptable level, a Chartered Accountant in public practice should decline to enter into the client relationship.
    4.1.6 Acceptance decisions should be periodically reviewed for recurring client engagements.
    4.2.0 Engagement Acceptance.
    4.2.1 A Chartered Accountant in public practice should agree to provide only those services that he is certified and competent to perform. Before accepting a specific client engagement, a Chartered Accountant in public practice should consider whether acceptance would create any threats to compliance with the fundamental principles. For example, a self-interest threat to professional competence and due care is created if the engagement team does not possess, or cannot acquire, the competencies necessary to properly carry out the engagement.
    4.2.2. A Chartered Accountant in public practice should evaluate the significance of identified threats and, if they are other than clearly insignificant, safeguards should be applied as necessary to eliminate them or reduce them to an acceptable level. Such safeguards may include but are not limited to:
    (a) Acquiring an appropriate understanding of the nature of the client's business, the complexity of its operations, the specific requirements of the engagement and the purpose, nature and scope of the work to be performed.
    (b) Acquiring knowledge of relevant industries or subject matters.
    (c) Assigning sufficient staff with the necessary competencies.
    (d) Using experts where necessary.
    (e)   Agreeing on a realistic time frame for the performance of the engagement.

(f) Complying with quality control policies and procedures designed to provide reasonable assurance that specific engagements are accepted, only when they can be performed competently.

4.2.3 When a Chartered Accountant in public practice intends to rely on the advice or work of an expert, he should evaluate whether such reliance is warranted, by considering factors such as reputation, expertise, resources available and applicable professional and ethical standards, information which may be gained from prior association with the expert or from consulting others.

4.2.4 Discussion Where an invitation to conduct a statutory audit comes other than directly from the client, the firm should first ensure that it has been properly appointed in accordance with statute and professional requirements. It should be made clear to all interested parties on all relevant documents that the member/firm is acting as principal, with all that the function implies. In those circumstances, the member should deal directly with the client and should render his own fee account.

4.3.0 Changes in a Professional Appointment.

4.3.1 A Chartered Accountant in public practice who is asked to replace another Chartered Accountant in public practice, or who is considering tendering for an engagement currently held by another Chartered Accountant in public practice, should determine whether there are any reasons, professional or otherwise for not accepting the engagement, such as circumstances that threaten compliance with the fundamental principles.

4.3.2 The significance of the threats should be evaluated depending on the nature of the engagement. This shall require direct communication with the existing Chartered Accountant to establish the facts and circumstances behind the proposed change so that the Chartered Accountant in public practice can decide whether or not it would be appropriate to accept the engagement. For example, the apparent reasons for the change in appointment may not fully reflect the facts and may indicate disagreements with the existing Chartered Accountant that may influence the decision as to whether or not to accept the appointment.

4.3.3 An existing Chartered Accountant is bound by confidentiality. The extent to which the Chartered Accountant in public practice can and should discuss the affairs of a client with a proposed Chartered Accountant will depend on the nature of the engagement and on:

(a) Whether or not the client's permission to do so has been obtained; or

(b) In the absence of specific instructions by the client, an existing Chartered Accountant should not ordinarily volunteer information about the client's affairs. Circumstances where it may be appropriate to disclose confidential information are set out in Paragraph 1.2.4 (h) of this Code.

4.3.4 Communication - The Procedure of 'Professional Enquiry ':

(i) The purpose of finding out the background to the proposed change is to enable the member to determine whether, in all the circumstances, it would be proper for him to accept the assignment. In particular, members nominated as auditors will wish to

ensure that they do not unwittingly become the means by which any unsatisfactory practice of the company or any impropriety in the conduct of its affairs may be enabled to continue or may be concealed from shareholders or other legitimately interested persons. Communication is meant to ensure that all relevant facts are known to the member who, having considered them, is then entitled to accept the nomination if he wishes so to do.

(ii) The need to communicate remains whether or not the existing Chartered Accountant in public practice or adviser intends to make representations to the proprietors, including his statutory right to make representations to the shareholders, and whether or not he still continues to act.

(iii) Communication of the facts to a prospective auditor or adviser cannot relieve the existing auditor or adviser of his duty to continue to impress on the client his views on any technical or ethical matters which may have led him into dispute with the client, nor does it affect the freedom of the client to exercise his right to a change of auditor or adviser.

4.3.5 When a member is first approached by a prospective client to act or be nominated, he should explain that he has a professional duty to communicate with the existing auditor or adviser.

38

4.3.6 When nominated or asked to act, the member should ask the client to inform the existing auditor or adviser of the proposed change and, at the same time, to give the latter written authority to discuss the client's affairs with the member. The member should then write to the existing Chartered Accountant or adviser, seeking information, which could influence his decision as to whether or not he may properly accept the appointment.

4.3.7 If the client fails or refuses to grant the existing Chartered Accountant or adviser permission to discuss the client's affairs with the proposed successor, the existing Chartered Accountant or adviser should report that fact to the prospective Chartered Accountant or adviser who should not accept nomination/appointment.

4.3.8 The existing Chartered Accountant or adviser should answer without delay the communication from the prospective Chartered Accountant. If there are no matters of which the latter should be aware, the existing Chartered Accountant or adviser should write to say that this is the case. If, however, there are such matters (see paragraph 4.3.16 below) he should inform the prospective successor of those facts within his knowledge of which, in his opinion, the latter should be aware. It is not sufficient to state that unspecified facts exist. The existing Chartered Accountant or adviser might prefer to explain these facts orally and the prospective Chartered Accountant or adviser should be prepared to confer with the existing Chartered Accountant or adviser if the latter so desires, and each should make his own record of such a discussion.

4.3.9 If an issue of conflicting viewpoints between the client and himself has been raised by the existing Chartered Accountant in his reply, the prospective successor should discuss the conflict with the client and satisfy himself either that the client's view is one which he can accept as reasonable or that the client will accept that the incoming chartered Accountant or adviser might have to express a contrary opinion.

4.3.10 Where the existing Chartered Accountant or adviser does not respond within a reasonable time, the prospective successor should endeavour to contact the existing Chartered Accountant by some other means, for instance, by telephone, facsimile or e-mail. Should this fail, and where the prospective successor has no reason to believe that there are untoward circumstances surrounding the change, he should send a final letter by recorded delivery service stating that unless he receives a reply within a specified time he will assume that there are no matters of which the existing Chartered Accountant is aware that should be brought to his attention. A member who accepts nomination in such circumstances is not precluded from complaining to the Institute that the existing Chartered Accountant did not respond to his enquiry letter.

4.3.11 If the prospective Chartered Accountant is satisfied that he can properly act, and is prepared to accept nomination/appointment, he should so inform the client in writing.

4.3.12 Where the member decides to accept nomination/appointment having been given notice of any matters, which are the subject of contention between the existing Chartered Accountant and the client, he should be prepared, if requested to do so, to demonstrate to the Institute that proper consideration has been given by him to those matters and that he believes that whatever threats exist they had been reduced to an acceptable level. Where the threats cannot be eliminated or reduced to an acceptable level through the application of safeguards, both the existing and the proposed incoming Chartered Accountant in public practice should, unless there is satisfaction as to necessary facts by other means, decline the engagement.

4.3.13 A Chartered Accountant in public practice may be asked to undertake work that is complementary or additional to the work of the existing Chartered Accountant. Such circumstances may give rise to potential threats of professional competence and due care resulting from, for example, a lack of or incomplete information. Safeguards against such threats include notifying the existing Chartered Accountant of the proposed work, which would give the existing Chartered Accountant the opportunity to provide any relevant information needed for the proper conduct of the work.

4.3.14 Statutory Provisions Firms must adhere to the statutory provisions relating to any change in an audit appointment especially those contained in Sections 362 to 366 of Companies and Allied Matters Act. Particularly the proposed Chartered Accountant should ensure that the previous Chartered Accountant has validly vacated office.

4.3.15 The matters referred to above with respect to questions on need to be aware of certain reasons why consent should not be granted that would, where relevant, include the following: (a) Reasons for the change advanced by the client of which the existing Chartered Accountant is aware are not in accordance with the facts (as understood by the latter); (b) The proposal to displace the existing Chartered Accountant arises in his *opinion because he has carried out his duties in the face of opposition or evasion(s) in which important differences of principle or practice had arisen with the client.*

(c) The client, its director, or employees may have been guilty of some unlawful act or default, or that any aspect of their conduct which is relevant to the carrying out of an audit or assignment ought, in the opinion of the existing Chartered Accountant to be investigated further by the appropriate authority;

(d) The existing Chartered Accountant has unconfirmed suspicions that the client or its directors or employees have defrauded the Revenue authorities (see paragraph 4.4.3. regarding privilege);

(e) The existing Chartered Accountant has serious doubts regarding the integrity of the directors and/or senior managers of the client company;

(f) The client, its directors, or employees have deliberately withheld information required by the existing Chartered Accountant or adviser for the performance of his duties or have limited or attempted to limit the scope of his work;

(g) The existing Chartered Accountant proposes to bring to the attention of members or creditors circumstances surrounding the proposed change of auditors in accordance with S.363 (1) (2) (a) (b) of the Companies and Allied Matters as amended.

4.3.16 The incumbent should neither refuse to communicate, nor delay his reply on the grounds that:-

(a) A prospective Auditor has obtained nomination in contravention of this guidance; or

(b) The incumbent Auditor has a genuine belief, whether justified or not, of having been unfairly treated by the client.

4.4.0 F u r t h e r P o i n t s - ' U n a c c e p t a b l e R e a s o n s '

4.4.1 Unpaid Fees   A member in public practice should not accept an audit assignment hitherto carried out by another member, without first ensuring that the other member has been properly removed from office as auditor and that all outstanding fees due to the other member have been fully paid.

4.4.2 C o n f i d e n t i a li t y   The prospective Auditor should ordinarily treat in confidence any information provided by the existing Auditor. However, it may be essential to the fulfillment of a prospective   Auditor's obligations that he should disclose such information. It may, for example, be unavoidable for the prospective Auditor to disclose to officers or employees of the client matters brought to his attention by the predecessor firm, which needs to be properly investigated. Such disclosure should be no wider than is necessary.

4.4.3 D e f a m a t i o n   It is likely that an existing Auditor who communicates to a prospective successor, matters damaging to the client or to any individual concerned with the client's business will have a strong measure of protection were any action for defamation to be brought against him, in that the communication will be protected by qualified privilege. This means that he should not be liable to pay damages for defamatory statements even if they turn out to be untrue, provided that they are made without malice. The chances of an incumbent being held to have acted maliciously are more provided that:

a) he states only what he sincerely believes to be true; and

b) he does not make reckless imputations against a client or individual connected with it which he can have no reason for believing to be true.

4.4.4 Joint Auditor A member whose firm is nominated as a Joint Auditor should communicate with all existing Auditors and be guided by similar principles to those set out in relation to nomination as an auditor. Where it is proposed that a joint audit appointment becomes a sole appointment, the surviving auditor should communicate formally with the outgoing joint auditor.

4.4.5 V a c a n c y A member whose firm is invited to accept nomination on the death of a sole practitioner Auditor should endeavour to obtain such information as he may need from the latter's alternative (where appropriate), the administrators of the estate or other sources.

4.4.6 T r a n s f e r o f B o o k s a n d P a p e r s A replaced auditor or adviser should transfer promptly to the client, or to his successor after the latter has been duly appointed, all books and papers which are in his possession and which belong to the client unless he is exercising a lien thereon for unpaid fees. Members should be aware that the courts have held that no lien can exist over books or documents of a registered company, which, e ither by statute or by article of association of the company, have to be available for public inspection. Members' attention is drawn to the Statement on fees. See paragraph 7.2 .0 on fees.

4.4.7 C o o p e r a t i o n w i t h a S u c c e s s o r The incoming Auditor often needs to ask his predecessor for information as to the client's affairs, lack of which might prejudice the client's interests. Such information should be promptly given and, unless there is good reason to the contrary, such as a significant amount of work involved, no charge should be made.

4.4.8 Additional Work A member invited to undertake recurring or non-recurring work, which is additional to and related to continuing work carried out by another Chartered Accountant or adviser should normally notify that other Chartered Accountant of the work he has been asked to undertake.

Discussion (a) It is generally in the interest of the client that the existing auditor be aware of the nature of the additional work being undertaken. The existing Chartered Accountant will be provided with the opportunity to communicate with the member to provide information, lack of which might otherwise prevent the additional work from being carried out effectively. Additionally, such notification could affect the way an existing Chartered Accountant discharges his continuing responsibilities to his client.

(b) Notification should always be given to the existing Chartered Accountant.

(c) Provision of all opinion on the application of accounting standards or principles clearly requires particular sensitivity to avoid adversarial positions between an Auditor and other Chartered Accountants wherever possible.

CHAPTER FIVE

5.0.0 CONFLICT OF INTEREST

5.1.1 A Chartered Accountant in public practice should take reasonable steps to identify circumstances that could pose a conflict of interest. Such circumstances may give rise to threats to compliance with the fundamental principles. For example, a threat to objectivity may be created when a Chartered Accountant in public practice competes directly with a client or has a joint venture or similar arrangement with a major competitor of a client. A threat to objectivity or confidentiality may also be created when a Chartered Accountant in public practice performs services for clients whose interests are in conflict or the clients are in dispute with each other in relation to the matter or transaction in question.

5.1.2 A Chartered Accountant in public practice should evaluate the significance of any threats. Evaluation includes considering, before accepting or continuing a client relationship or specific engagement, whether the Chartered Accountant in public practice has any business interests, or relationships with the client or a third party that could give rise to threats. If threats are other than clearly insignificant, safeguards should be considered and applied as necessary to eliminate them or reduce them to an acceptable level.

5.1.3 The following additional safeguards should also be considered:

(a) The use of separate engagement teams.

(b) Procedures to prevent access to information (e.g. strict physical separation of such teams, confidential and secure data filing).

(c) Clear guidelines for members of the engagement team on issues of security and confidentiality.

(d) The use of confidentiality agreements signed by employees and partners of the firm.

(e) Regular review of the application of safeguards by a senior individual not involved with relevant client engagements.

5.1.4 Where a conflict of interest poses a threat to one or more of the fundamental principles, including objectivity, confidentiality or professional behaviour that cannot be eliminated or reduced to an acceptable level through the application of safeguards, the Chartered

Accountant in public practice should conclude that it is not appropriate to accept a specific engagement or that resignation from one or more conflicting engagements is required.

5.1.5 Where a Chartered Accountant in public practice has requested consent from a client to act for another party (which may or may not be an existing client) in respect of a matter where the respective interests are in conflict and that consent has been with-held by the client, then they must not continue to act for one of the parties in the matter giving rise to the conflict of interest.

CHAPTER SIX
6.0.0 SECOND OPINIONS

    6.1.0 Situations where a Chartered Accountant in public practice is asked to provide a second opinion on the application of accounting and taxation, auditing, reporting or other standards or principles to specific circumstances or transactions by or on behalf of a company or an entity that is not an existing client may give rise to threats to compliance with the fundamental principles. For example, there may be a threat to professional competence and due care in circumstances where the second opinion is not based on the same set of facts that were made available to the existing Chartered Accountant, or is based on an inadequate evidence. The significance of the threat will depend on the circumstances of the request and all the other available facts and assumptions relevant to the expression of a professional opinion.

    6.1.1 When asked to provide such an opinion, a Chartered Accountant in public practice should evaluate the significance of the threats and if they are other than clearly insignificant, safeguards should be considered and applied as necessary to eliminate or reduce them to an acceptable level. Such safeguards may include seeking client permission to access all relevant information from the existing Chartered Accountant or other source.

    6.1.2 If the company or entity seeking the opinion will not permit communication with the existing Chartered Accountant, a Chartered Accountant in public practice should decline the engagement.

CHAPTER SEVEN
7.0.0 PROFESSIONAL FEES AND OTHER TYPES OF REMUNERATION

    This Statement applies only to practising members, affiliates and, where appropriate, employees of practising firms.

    7.1.0 Introductory Note The Institute states that a member is entitled to charge for his services.

    (a) such specific fee as agreed with the client or; (b) a fee calculated in accordance with any agreement with the client; or (c) in the absence of an agreement, a fee calculated by reference to the custom of the profession or in accordance with regulations of the Institute in force at the time the fees were charged.

    7.1.1 In the last event it is customary, where the basis of the fee has not been agreed with a client, that a member should charge a fee which is fair and reasonable having regard to:

    (a) the seniority and professional expertise of the persons necessarily engaged in the work;

    (b) the time expended by each;

    (c) the degree of risk and responsibility which the work entails; (d) the priority and importance of the work to the client together with any expenses properly incurred.

7.1.2

The Institute's minimum charge-out rates in respect of fees for professional services are intended to set a benchmark for such fees below which members are not ordinarily expected to charge.

7.1.3 When entering into negotiations regarding professional services, a Chartered Accountant in public practice may quote whatever fee deemed to be appropriate. A self interest threat to professional competence and due care is created if the fee quoted is so low that it may be difficult to perform the engagement in accordance with applicable technical and professional standards for that price.

47

7.1.4 A Chartered Accountant in public practice may receive a referral fee or commission relating to a client as well as a commission from a third party (e.g., a software vendor) in connection with the sale of goods or services to a client. However accepting such a referral fee or commission may give rise to self-interest threats to objectivity, and professional competence and due care.

7.1.5 A Chartered Accountant in public practice shall not pay or receive a referral fee to obtain a client, for example, where the client continues as a client of another Chartered Accountant in public practice but requires specialist services not offered by the existing Chartered Accountant. The payment of such a referral fee may also create a self-interest threat to objectivity and professional competence and due care.

7.1.6 A Chartered Accountant in public practice may purchase all or part of another firm on the basis that payments will be made to individuals formerly owning the firm or to their heirs or estates. Such payments are not regarded as commissions or referral fees for the purpose of this paragraph.

7.2.0

Fee Quotation and Estimates. A member should inform a client in writing prior to commencement of any engagement the basis upon which any fee he proposes to charge for his services will be calculated and, on request and where practicable, the level of fees likely to be charged for any assignment.

7.2.1 Discussion The member should, at the earliest opportunity, discuss and explain the basis on which fees will be calculated and, where practicable, the estimated initial fee. The arrangements agreed should be confirmed in writing, normally in an engagement letter, including a confirmation on any estimate, quotation or other indicators, and where the basis of future fees will differ from that of initial fees, the basis on which such fees will be rendered. Where there is no engagement letter, the member should confirm the initial discussion in writing to the client as soon as practicable.

7.2.2 Fee proposals should be made only after proper consideration of the nature of the client's business, the complexity of its operation and the work to be performed.

7.2.3 The fact that a member has quoted a fee lower than another is not improper provided care is taken to ensure that the client has a full and complete understanding of.

(a) the services to be covered by the fee; and (b) the basis on which the fee is to be determined both for the current and future years.

7.2.4   Audit Work Firms should not quote for new work a level of fees which is lower than that charged by an existing auditor or quote by tender, levels of fees which they have reason to believe are significantly lower than those quoted by other tendering firms as their objectivity could in those circumstances be threatened. Such firms should ensure that their work complies with Auditing Standards and Guidelines and, in particular, quality control procedures. In the event of a complaint being made to the Institute (which might have arisen as a result of a Professional Practice Monitoring Committee's inspection), where fees were a feature in obtaining or retaining the work, firms should be prepared to demonstrate that:

(a) the work done was in accordance with Auditing Standards; and

(b) the client was not misled as to the basis on which fees for the current and subsequent years were to be determined.

7.3.0 Fee Information and Disputes A member should furnish, either in the fee account or subsequently on request, and without further charge, such details as are reasonable to enable the client to understand the basis on which the fee account has been prepared.

7.3.1 Where fees rendered exceed, without prior agreement, a quotation or estimate or indication of fees given by a member by more than a reasonable amount, the member should be prepared to provide the client with a full explanation of the excess and to take steps to resolve speedily any dispute which arises.

7.3.2 A member whose fees have not been paid may be entitled to retain certain books and papers of a client upon which he has been working by exercising a lien and may refuse to pass on information to the client or his successor Chartered Accountant, until those fees are paid. However, a member who so acts should be prepared to take reasonable steps to resolve any dispute relating to the amount of that fee. The incoming Auditor has a duty to assist in the recovery of such fees within a reasonable time.

7.4.0   Percentage and Contingent Fees Unless the circumstances dictate otherwise or the client clearly objects fees should normally be charged on time rates in respect of audit work, reporting assignment and similar non-audit roles. In all circumstances, a member in public practice should refrain from quoting or charging fees for assurance work, reporting assignment and similar non assurance roles using criteria other than the basis or bases approved by the Institute.

7.4.1 Discussion In bankruptcies, liquidations, receiverships, administrations, voluntary arrangements and similar work the remuneration may, by statute or tradition, be based on a percentage of realizations or a percentage of distribution. Consequently, it may not be possible to negotiate a fee in advance or base it on the principle in paragraph 7.4.0 above.

7.4.2 In some circumstances, such as advising on a management buy-out, the raising of venture capital, acquisition search or sales mandates, fees cannot realistically be charged save on a contingency basis; to require otherwise would, in certain cases, deprive potential clients of professional assistance, for example where the capacity of the client to pay is dependent upon the success or failure of the venture.

7.4.3 Where work is subject to a fee on a contingency, percentage or similar basis, the capacity in which a member has worked and the basis of his remuneration should be made clear in any document prepared by the member in contemplation that a third party may rely on it.

CHAPTER EIGHT
8.0.0 MARKETING PROFESSIONAL SERVICES.

8.1.0 When a Chartered Accountant in public practice solicits new work through advertising or other forms of marketing, there may be potential threats to compliance with the fundamental principles. For example, a self-interest threat to compliance with the principle of professional behaviour is created if services, achievements or products are marketed in a way that is inconsistent with the principle.

8.1.1 A Chartered Accountant in public practice should not bring the profession into disrepute when marketing professional services. The Chartered Accountant in public practice should be honest and truthful and should not:

(a) make exaggerated claims for services offered, qualifications possessed or experience gained; or

(b) make disparaging references to unsubstantiated comparisons to the work of another Chartered Accountant.

If the Chartered Accountant in public practice is in doubt whether a proposed form of advertising or marketing is appropriate, the Chartered Accountant in public practice should consult through the Registrar/Chief Executive of the Institute of Chartered Accountants of Nigeria.

CHAPTER NINE
9.0.0 THE NAMES AND LETTERHEADS OF PRACTISING FIRMS

9.1.0 For the purpose of interpretation, the term 'firm' includes a partnership, and a sole practitioner, the main business of which is the provision of services customarily provided by chartered accountants, while the term 'letterhead' means any part of the firm's notepaper and documents used by the firm for communicating with clients or other parties.

9.1.1 Subject to the following guidance, a member in public practice should refrain from practising in or under a name which does not comprise proper name(s) only, such name(s) being that or those of one or more of the current or former proprietor(s) and/or partner(s) of the Firm.

9.1.2 A practice name shall be consistent with the dignity of the profession in the sense that it shall not project an image inconsistent with that of a professional practice bound to high ethical and technical standards.

9.1.3 A practice name shall not be misleading.

9.1.4 D i s c u s s i o n (a) It would be misleading for a firm with very few offices to describe itself as 'international' merely on the ground that one of them was overseas. Similarly, it would be misleading for a sole practitioner to add the suffix 'and Associates' to the name of his practice unless formal arrangements were agreed with two or more consultants or firms.

(b) A practice name would be misleading if in all the circumstances there was a real risk that it could be confused with the name of another firm, even if the member(s) of the practice could lay justifiable claim to the name.

(c) It has been the custom of the profession for members to practice under a firm's name based on the names of past or present members of the firm itself or of a firm with which it has merged or amalgamated. A practice name so derived will usually be in conformity with this Code of ethics

(d) There is no objection to membership of a practicing group being indicated on the firm's notepaper or elsewhere in proximity to the practice name. However, the name of such a firm should be clearly distinguishable from the name of an associated firm or group. Thus, it would be misleading for a member of a practicing group to bear the same name as the group, but there could be no objection to a firm practicing under its own name 'as a member' of (a named) accountancy group.

9.1.5 U s e o f t h e D e s c r i p t i o n 'C h a r t e r e d A c c o u n t a n t s ' a) Use of the description 'Chartered Accountants' is governed by the law establishing the Institute i.e. the ICAN Act . A Chartered Accountant in public practice must have all member partners to enable the firm describe itself (practice) as "Chartered Accountants".

b) Firms entitled to use the description 'Chartered Accountants are encouraged to do so, on their letterheads, in advertisements and generally. A firm, which describes itself as 'Chartered Accountants' on its notepaper may include a list of the services it particularly wishes to offer.

9.1.6 D i s c u s s i o n : L e g a l R e q u i r e m e n t s A practice letterhead must comply with partnership and company law as appropriate.

9.1.7 D i s c u s s i o n : O v e r s e a s F i r m s Overseas firms are required to comply with any local laws as to practice names so far as overseas offices are concerned. Subject thereto, they may describe themselves in any manner conformable to the practice of the profession locally provided that the principles set out in the paragraphs 9.1.2-9.1.5 above are observed.

9.1.8 D i s c u s s i o n : N e w a n d C h a n g e d N a m e s Save where the name of a firm is based on the names of past or present members of the firm itself or of a firm with which it has merged or amalgamated, when a new firm is to be set up and when it is desired to change the name of an existing firm, members are advised, as a means of ensuring compliance with these rules, to consult the Institute as to the propriety of the proposed name.

9.1.9 P e r s o n s N a m e d o n L e t t e r h e a d s (a) It should be clear from the letterhead of a practice whether any person named thereon, other than persons named only in the name of the firm, is a partner of the practice.

(b) No person named on the letterhead of a practice should be described by a title, description or designatory letters to which he or she is not entitled.

CHAPTER TEN
10.0.0   GIFTS AND HOSPITALITY
        10.1.0 A Chartered Accountant in public practice, or an immediate or close family member, may be offered gifts and hospitality from a client. However such an offer ordinarily gives rise to threats to compliance with the fundamental principles. For example, self-interest threats to objectivity may be created if a gift from a client is accepted; intimidation threats to objectivity may result from the possibility of such offers being made public.

        10.1.1 The nature, value and intent behind the offer, determine the significance of the threat therein. Where gifts or hospitality which a reasonable and informed third party, having knowledge of all relevant information, would consider clearly insignificant are made to a Chartered Accountant in public practice may conclude that the offer is made in the normal course of business without the specific intent to influence decision making or to obtain information. In such cases, the Chartered Accountant in public practice may generally conclude that there is no significant threat to compliance with the fundamental principles.

CHAPTER ELEVEN
11.0.0   CUSTODY OF CLIENT ASSETS
        11.1.1 A Chartered Accountant in public practice should not assume custody of client monies or other assets unless permitted to do so by law and, if so, in compliance with any additional legal duties imposed on a Chartered Accountant in public practice holding such assets.

        11.1.2 The holding of client assets creates threats to compliance with the fundamental principles; for example, there is self-interest threat to professional behavior and may be a self-interest threat to objectivity arising from holding client assets. To safeguard against such threats, a Chartered Accountant in public practice entrusted with money (or other assets) belonging to others should:
        (a) Keep such assets separately from personal or firm assets;
        (b) Use such assets only for the purpose for which they are intended;
        (c) At all times, be ready to account for those assets, and any income, dividends or any gains generated, to any persons entitled to such accounting;
        (d) Comply with all relevant laws and regulations relevant to the holding of and accounting for such assets.
        11.1.2 In addition, a Chartered Accountant in public practice should be aware of threats to compliance with the fundamental principles through association with such assets, for example, if the assets were found to derive from illegal activities, such as money laundering or obtaining by false pretenses. As part of client and engagement acceptance procedures for such services the Chartered Accountant in public practice should make

appropriate inquiries about the source of such assets and should consider their legal and regulatory obligations. They should also seek legal advice, if in doubt.

CHAPTER TWELVE
12.0.0   INDEPENDENCE–ASSURANCE ENGAGEMENTS
        12.1.0 Objective and Structure of this chapter
        12.1.1 The objective of this chapter is to assist firms and members of assurance teams in:
        (a) Identifying threats to independence;
        (b) Evaluating whether these threats are clearly insignificant
        In cases where the threats are not clearly insignificant, identifying and applying appropriate safeguards to eliminate or reduce the threats to an acceptable level. Consideration should always be given to what a reasonable and informed third party having knowledge of all relevant information, including safeguards applied, would reasonably conclude to be unacceptable. In situations when no safeguards are available to reduce the threat to an acceptable level, the only possible actions are to eliminate the activities or interest creating the threat, or to refuse to accept or refuse to continue the assurance engagement.

        12.2.0 This chapter concludes with some examples of how this conceptual approach to independence is to be applied to specific circumstances and relationships. The examples discuss threats to independence that may be created by specific circumstances and relationships (paragraphs 12.4.0 onwards). Professional judgment is used to determine the appropriate safeguards to eliminate threats to independence or to reduce them to an acceptable level. In certain examples, the threats to independence are so significant, the only possible actions are to eliminate the activities or interest creating the threat, or to refuse to accept or continue the assurance engagement. In other examples, the threat can be eliminated or reduced to an acceptable level by the application of safeguards. The examples are not intended to be exhaustive.

        12.3.0 Certain examples in this section indicate how the framework is to be applied to a financial statements audit engagement for a quoted entity. When a firm chooses not to differentiate between quoted entities and other entities, the examples that relate to financial statement audit engagements for quoted entities should be considered to apply to all financial statement audit engagements.

        12.4.0 When threats to independence are not clearly insignificant, the firm can decide to accept or continue the assurance engagement. This decision should be documented and should include a description of the threats identified and the safeguards applied to eliminate or reduce the threats to an acceptable level.

        56

        12.5.0 The evaluation of the significance of any threats to independence and the safeguards necessary to reduce any threat to an acceptable level, takes into account the public interest. Certain entities may be of significant public interest as a result of their business and their size, their corporate status and their wide range of stakeholders.

Examples of such entities may include quoted companies, financial institutions, insurance companies, and pension funds. Because of the strong public interest in the financial statements of quoted entities, certain paragraphs in this section deal with additional matters that are relevant to the financial statement audit of quoted entities. Consideration should be given to the application of the framework in relation to the financial statement audit of quoted entities to other financial statement audit clients that may be of significant public interest.

   12.6.0 Corporate governance is enhanced where the independence of client management assist the Board of Directors in satisfying themselves that a firm is independent in carrying out its audit role. There should be regular communication between the firm and the audit committee (or other governance body if there is no audit committee) of quoted entities regarding relationships and other matters that might, in the firm's opinion, reasonably be thought to bear on independence.

   12.7.0 Firms should establish policies and procedures relating to independence, Communications with audit committees, or others charged with governance of the client. In the case of the financial statement audit of quoted entities, the firm should communicate orally and in writing at least annually, all relationships and other matters between the firm, network firms and the financial statement audit client that in the firm's professional judgment may reasonably be thought to bear on independence. Matters to be communicated will vary in each circumstance and should be decided by the firm, but should generally address the relevant matters set out in this section.

CHAPTER THIRTEEN
13.0.0   ASSERTION BASED - ASSURANCE ENGAGEMENT   In the case of an assertion based assurance engagement it is in the public interest and, therefore, required by this Code of Ethics, that members of assurance teams, firms and where applicable, network firms be independent of assurance clients.

   13.1.0 In an assertion based assurance engagement, the Chartered Accountant in public practice expresses a conclusion designed to enhance the degree of confidence of the intended users other than the responsible party about the outcome of the evaluation or measurement of a subject matter against criteria.

   13.1.1 Assurance engagements may be assertion-based or direct reporting. In either case they involve three separate parties: a Chartered Accountant in public practice, a responsible party and intended users.

   13.1.2 In an assertion-based assurance engagement, which includes a financial statement audit engagement, the evaluation or measurement of the subject matter is performed by the responsible party, and the subject matter information is in the form of an assertion by the responsible party that is made available to the intended users.

   13.1.3 In a direct reporting assurance engagement the Chartered Accountant in public practice either directly performs the evaluation or measurement of the subject matter, or obtains a representation from the responsible party that has performed the *evaluation or measurement that is not available to the intended users. The subject matter information is provided to the intended users in the assurance report.*

13.2.0 Independence

13.2.1 Independence of Mind

The state of mind that permits the expression of a conclusion without being affected by influences that compromise professional judgment, allowing an individual to act with integrity, and exercise objectivity and professional skepticism.

13.2.2

Independence in Appearance The avoidance of facts and circumstances that are so significant that a reasonable and informed third party, having knowledge of all relevant information, including safeguards applied, would reasonably conclude a firm's, or a member of the assurance team's, integrity, objectivity or professional skepticism had been compromised.

13.2.3   The use of the word "independence" on its own may create misunderstandings. Standing alone, the word may lead observers to suppose that a person exercising professional judgment ought to be free from all economic, financial and other relationships. This is impossible, as every member of society has relationships with others. Therefore, the significance of economic, financial and other relationships should also be evaluated in the light of what a reasonable and informed third party having knowledge of all relevant information would reasonably conclude to be unacceptable.

13.2.4   A conceptual framework that requires firms and members of assurance teams to identify, evaluate and address threats to independence, rather than merely comply with a set of specific rules, which may be arbitrary, is, therefore, in the public interest. An exhaustive list of situations that create threats cannot be provided. However a conceptual framework to include but not limited to the following: frame works are listed below.

13.3.0 A Conceptual Approach to Independence

13.3.1 Members of assurance teams, firms and network firms are required to apply the conceptual framework contained in part 1 (Fundamental Principles) to the particular circumstances under consideration. In addition to identifying relationships between the firm, network firms, members of the assurance team and the assurance client, consideration should be given to whether or not relationships between individuals outside of the assurance team and the assurance client create threats to independence.

13.3.2 The examples presented in this section are intended to illustrate the application of the conceptual framework and are not intended to be, nor should they be interpreted as, an exhaustive list of all circumstances that may create threats to independence. Consequently, it is not sufficient for a member of an assurance team, a firm or a network firm merely to comply with the examples presented, rather they should apply the framework to the particular circumstances they face.

13.3.3 The nature of the threats to independence and the applicable safeguards necessary to eliminate the threats or reduce them to an acceptable level differ depending on the characteristics of the individual assurance engagement: whether or not it is a financial statement audit engagement or another type of assurance engagement; and in the latter case, the purpose, subject matter information and intended users of the report. A firm should, therefore, evaluate the relevant circumstances, the nature of the assurance engagement and the threats to independence in deciding whether or not it is appropriate to accept or continue an engagement, as well as the nature of the safeguards required and if a particular individual should be a member of the assurance team.

13.4.0 Comments On Assertion-based Assurance Engagements

13.4.1 Financial statement audit engagements are relevant to a wide range of potential users; consequently, in addition to independence of mind, independence in appearance is of particular significance. Accordingly, for financial statement audit clients, the members of the assurance team, the firm and network firms are required to be independent of the financial statement audit client. Such independence requirements include prohibitions regarding certain relationships between members of the assurance team and directors, officers and employees of the client in a position to exert direct and significant influence over the subject matter information (the financial statements). Also, consideration should be given to whether threats to independence are created by relationships with employees of the client in a position to exert direct and significant influence over the subject matter (the financial position, financial performance and cash flows).

13.4.2 Other Assertion-based Assurance Engagements   In an assertion-based assurance engagement where the client is not a financial statement audit client, the members of the assurance team and the firm are required to be independent of the assurance client (the responsible party, which is responsible for the subject matter information and may be responsible for the subject matter). Such independence requirements include prohibitions regarding certain relationships between members of the assurance team and directors, officers and employees of the client in a position to exert direct and significant influence over the subject matter information. Also, consideration should be given to whether threats to independence are created by relationships with employees of the client in a position to exert direct and significant influence over the subject matter of the engagement. Consideration should also be given to any threats that the firm has reason to believe may be created by network firm interests and relationships.

13.4.3 In the majority of assertion-based assurance engagements, that are not financial statement audit engagements, the responsible party is responsible for the subject matter information and the subject matter. However, in some engagements the responsible party may not be responsible for the subject matter. For example, when a Chartered Accountant in public practice is engaged to perform an assurance engagement regarding a report that an environmental consultant has prepared about a company's sustainability practices, for distribution to intended users, the environmental consultant is the responsible party for the subject matter information but the company is responsible for the subject matter (Environmental impact assessment).

13.4.4 In those assertion-based assurance engagements that are not financial statement audit engagements, where the responsible party is responsible for the subject matter information but not the subject matter, the members of the assurance team and the firm are required to be independent of the party responsible for the subject matter information (the assurance client). In addition, consideration should be given to any threats the firm has reason to believe may be created by interests and relationships between a member of the assurance team, the firm, a network firm and the party responsible for the subject matter.

13.4.5 Direct Reporting Assurance Engagements
In a direct reporting assurance engagement the members of the assurance team and the firm are required to be independent of the assurance client (the party responsible for the subject matter).

CHAPTER FOURTEEN
14.0.0 RESTRICTED USE REPORTS
14.1.0 *In the case of an assurance report in respect of a non-financial statement audit client expressly restricted for use by identified users, the users of the report are considered to be knowledgeable as to the purpose, subject matter information and limitations of the report through their participation in establishing the nature and scope of the firm's instructions to deliver the services as in the terms of reference. Details of the terms of reference should highlight any threats upon review by the users. If the firm had a material financial interest, whether direct or indirect, in the assurance client, the self-interest threat created would be so significant no safeguard could reduce the threat to an acceptable level therefore the job should not be accepted.*

CHAPTER FIFTEEN
15.0.0 MULTIPLE RESPONSIBLE PARTIES
15.1.1 *In some assurance engagements, whether assertion-based or direct reporting, that are not financial statement audit engagements, there might be several responsible parties. In such engagements, in determining whether it is necessary to apply the provisions in this section to each responsible party, the firm may take into account whether an interest or relationship between the firm, or a member of the assurance team, and a particular responsible party would create a threat to independence that is other than clearly insignificant in the context of the subject matter information. This will take into account factors such as:*
(a) The materiality of the subject matter information (or the subject matter) for which the particular responsible party is responsible; and
(b) The degree of public interest associated with the engagement. If the firm determines that the threat to independence created by any such interest or relationship with a particular responsible party would be clearly insignificant it may not be necessary to apply all of the provisions of this section to that responsible party.

15.2.0 Other Considerations In the case of a financial statement audit client, the threats, safeguards including independence applicable to an assurance client are also applicable to related entities where the assurance client is a quoted entity.

15.2.1 the evaluation of threats to independence and subsequent action should be supported by evidence obtained before accepting the engagement and while it is being performed, this obligation to evaluate arises when a firm, or a member of the assurance team knows, or could reasonably be expected to know, of circumstances that might compromise independence.

15.2.2 throughout this chapter, reference is made to significant and clearly insignificant threats in the evaluation of independence. In considering the significance of any particular matter, qualitative as well as quantitative factors should be taken into account. A matter should be considered clearly insignificant only if it is deemed to be both trivial and inconsequential.

15.3.0 Engagement Period

15.3.1 The members of the assurance team and the firm should be independent of the assurance client during the period of the assurance engagement. The period of the engagement starts in the case of the financial audit client, when the firm is appointed or re-appointed at the Annual General Meeting (AGM). In the case of the non-financial audit client, the engagement begins when they are appointed to perform a specific assignment, and ends at the issuance of the final assurance report.

15.3.2 In the case of a financial statement audit engagement, the engagement period includes the period covered by the financial statements reported on by the firm. When an entity becomes a financial statement audit client during or after the period covered by the financial statements that the firm will report on, the firm should consider whether any threats to independence may be created by:

(a) Financial or business relationships with the audit client during or after the period covered by the financial statements, but prior to the acceptance of the financial statement audit engagement; or

(b) Previous services provided to the audit client. Similarly, with non-financial statement audit engagement, the firm should consider whether any financial or business relationships or previous services may create threats to independence. It is imperative that the statutory provisions, relating to any change in an audit appointment, in particular those contained in Sections 362 to 366 of Companies and Allied Matters Act 1990, and in particular that the proposed auditor should ensure that the previous auditor has validly vacated office, be adhered to.

15.3.3 A non-assurance service provided to an un-quoted financial statement audit client will not impair the firm's independence when the client becomes a quoted entity provided:

(a) The previous non-assurance service was permissible under this section for unquoted financial statement and clients.

(b) The service will be terminated within a reasonable period of time of the client becoming quoted entity, if they are impermissible under this section for financial statement audit client that are quoted entities and

(c) The firm has implemented appropriate safeguards to eliminate any threats to independence arising from the previous service or reduce them to an acceptable level.

CHAPTER SIXTEEN
16.0.0 GUIDANCE ON SOME SPECIFIC ISSUES
INTRODUCTION:
The examples below describe specific circumstances and relationships that may create threats to the fundamental principles, the safeguards that may be appropriate to eliminate them or reduce them to an acceptable level in each circumstance. The examples are not all inclusive, however they illustrate how the framework applies to assurance clients. The examples should be read in conjunction with Parts Two and Three of this code.

16.1.0 Guidance on specific areas of threat:

16.1.1 Area of Risk – Undue Dependence on an Assurance Client   (a) A new firm seeking to establish itself or an established firm   reducing its activities may not be able to comply with the 25% minimum criteria, at any event in the short term. Such firms should take particular care to implement the safeguards referred to in (c) below.

(b)   Individual engagement partners within a firm may also be faced with a personal threat because their personal portfolio is dominated by a single client, on whom they might become so dependent as to lose their objectivity.   (c)   The fees from a number of one-off assignments could   contribute to a problem of undue dependence. One-off assignments, which by their special and repetitive nature become regular assignments, should be regarded on the same basis as recurring fees.

16.1.2 Safeguards in relation to undue dependence on an audi t client   (a) A member shall not accept an audit appointment or similar reporting assignment from an entity, which regularly provides him, his firm or an office within the firm with an unduly large proportion of his or its gross practice income. An unduly large proportion would normally be 25 per cent.   (b) Where a member is dependent for his income on the profits of any one office within a firm and the gross income of that office is regularly dependent on one client or a group of connected clients for more than 25 per cent of its gross fees, a partner from another office should take final responsibility for any report

(c) In addition to paragraph 3.3.2 the Chartered Accountant should be aware that the discussion therein, indicates only the extreme beyond which the public perception of a member's objectivity is likely to be at risk. It is the duty of the firm regularly to satisfy itself that it is not open to criticism in respect of any audit engagement, having regard to all the circumstances of the case. For this purpose a firm should, before accepting an audit appointment and as part of its annual review, carefully consider against the criteria set out in this Statement the propriety of accepting or retaining each audit client or group of connected clients the fees from which for audit and other recurring work, excluding one-off

assignments, represent 25 per cent or more of the gross practice income or of the gross earned income of a member practicing part time.

    16.1.3 Area of risk - Loans to or from a client ; guarantees ; overdue fees

    (a) A self-interest threat will arise if an audit firm or any principal of the firm should directly or indirectly make any loan to, or receive a loan from, a client or give or accept any guarantee in relation to a debt of the client, firm or principal.

    (b) An audit firm or a principal of the firm should not receive any loan from a client. This is because the size of the perceived self-interest threat arising in such circumstance is generally seen as being too great to be offset by all available safeguards, where a firm or principal makes any loan to a client. This restriction does not normally apply to accounts in credit with a client-clearing bank or similar financial institution.

    (c) The above paragraph is not intended to prevent a loan, overdraft or home mortgage being accepted from an audit- client financial institution in the normal course of business and all normal commercial terms by a principal or employee, unless: (i) the loan is applied so as to subscribe to partnership capital; or   (ii) the principal is an engagement partner in relation to the client.

    (d) Overdue fees   Similar considerations as in (c) above apply where there are significant overdue fees from a client or group of connected clients.

    (e) Safeguards in relation to overdue fees Before work is commenced on an audit where there are overdue fees, a review of the situation should be undertaken by a principal not involved in the audit to ascertain whether the overdue fees, taken together with the fees for the current assignment, could be regarded as a significant loan. Where the fee is material or significant, the self-interest threat created would be so significant that no safeguard could reduce it to an acceptable level.

    16.1.4   Area of risk - hospitality or other benefits A self-interest threat and familiarity threat arises where anyone in the firm receives a benefit by way of goods or services or hospitality from a client.

    16.1.5 SAFEGUARD Gifts or hospitality should not, therefore, be accepted by a firm or by anyone closely connected with it unless the value of any such benefit is clearly insignificant, otherwise threats to independence cannot be reduced to an acceptable level

    16.1.6 Area of risk - actual or threatened litigation   (a) Where litigation takes place, or appears likely to take place, between an audit firm and a client, both a self-interest threat and an intimidation threat may arise.

    (b) These threats are likely to call into question the objectivity of the auditor and his ability to report fairly and impartially on the company's accounts. At the same time, the existence of such action or threat of action could affect the willingness of the management of the company to disclose necessary information to the auditor.

    (c) The issue by the client of a writ for negligence against the auditor would be considered to impair the latter's objectivity. The inclusion in any litigation of allegations against the client of fraud or deceit made by the auditor may also impair objectivity. Such impairment may not necessarily result when the litigation arises solely out of a fee dispute.

(d) It is not possible to specify precisely the point at which it would become improper for a firm to continue as auditors.

16.1.7 SAFEGUARDS A firm should have regard to circumstances where the public might perceive litigation, e.g. where publicity is given to matters adversely affecting a quoted or other public interest company and reference is made to the company's reliance on accounts or other financial statements prepared by the firm. Once the significance of the threat has been evaluated, the following should be applied to reduce the threat to an acceptable level:

(a) Disclose to the audit committee or others charged with governance, the extent and nature of the litigation;

(c) If the litigation involves a member of the Assurance team, remove the individual from the team;

(d) Involve an additional Chartered Accountant in the Firm who was not a member of the assurance team, to review the work done and advise as necessary.   If the safeguards above do not reduce the threat to an appropriate level, the only option available to the Firm is to withdraw from, or refuse to accept the assurance engagement.

16.1.8 Area of risk - Participation in the affairs of a client. Participation in the affairs of a client is likely to lead to self-interest threats, which are either in practice too great to be over-ridden by available safeguards, or is likely to appear so to interested parties.

Self-interest threats can also arise if an officer or senior employee of an audit client is closely connected to the principal of the audit firm. For the purposes of this paragraph only, the definition of "closely connected includes, also adult children and their spouses, brothers and sisters; their spouses, and any relative to whom regular financial assistance is given or who is otherwise indebted financially to the principal.

16.1.9 SAFEGUARD

(a) There are statutory prohibitions on a firm acting as auditor. For instance, Section 358 (2) of the Companies and Allied Matters Act, 1990 as amended prohibits an officer or employee of a company or a partner an employee of such a person, from accepting appointment as auditor of that company.

(b) In general, no principal or employee of an audit firm may be an officer or employee of a client, and should not have held such a position in a period so closely preceding the firm's appointment as to constitute a significant threat of self-interest or self-review.

(c) A member should not personally take part in the conduct of the audit of a company if he has, during the period upon which the report is to be made or at any time in the two years prior to the first day thereof, been an officer (other than auditor) or employee of that company.

16.1.10 Area of risk - principal or senior employee joining client   (a) The objectivity of a firm reporting on a company (or other entity) may be threatened, or appear to be threatened, if an officer of the audit client has been a principal or senior employee of the firm.

(b) *Threats to the firm's objectivity of a self-interest nature may arise where there remain significant connections between the officer and his former firm, and appropriate action should be taken to ensure that objectivity is not impaired. For example:*

(i) *the officer should not derive retirement or other benefits from the firm unless these are made in accordance with pre-determined arrangements that cannot be influenced by any remaining connections between the officer and his former firm. In addition, any amount owed should not be such as to appear likely to threaten the firm's objectivity; and*

(ii) *the officer should not participate or appear to participate in the firm's business or professional activities. Inclusion on the notepaper of the firm is an indication of such participation and the provision of office accommodation or secretarial or information technology support by the firm may indicate such participation.*

(c)   *Additionally, the firm's objectivity may be threatened because of participation in the conduct of an audit by a principal or senior employee in the knowledge that he is to join the client.*

16.1.11   *Safeguards in relation to principal or senior employee joining audit client   The firm should make appropriate provisions in its procedures for further safeguards to include compliance with the relevant provision of the labour law.*

16.1.12 *Area of risk - beneficial interest in shares and other investments. Shares and Shareholdings.   Reference to shares and shareholdings should be taken to include debenture and   other Loan stock and the equivalent, and rights to acquire shares, debenture or other loan stock. Shareholdings also include options to purchase or sell such securities. A person's holdings include holdings by a nominee on behalf of that person or by a trust created by that person for his or her personal benefit. Shareholdings in parent, subsidiary or associated companies of a Client Company should normally be regarded on the same basis as shareholdings in the Client Company itself. However, if the firm is an auditor only of a Company or Companies which, taken together, constitute an insignificant part of a group, independence of the parent Company, etc is not required.*

16.1.13   *SAFEGUARDS   (a) Where an employee, or a person closely connected with an employee, has such a beneficial interest, the employee should not take part in the audit of the client company.   (b) A principal in an audit firm may invest in unit trusts or in an Investment trust, provided that the firm does not report upon the trust.*

(c) *Where a principal inherits shares or marries a shareholder, or a relevant investment occurs as a result of a take-over, the investment should be disposed of at the earliest practicable date, being a date at which the transaction would not amount to insider dealing. Similar action should be taken where a beneficial investment is held in a company becoming an audit client. Where the necessary disposal cannot be achieved within the time scale envisaged, the firm should not continue as auditor.*

16.1.14 *Area of risk - trusteeships*

(a) *If a principal or employee of the firm or a person closely connected with it either acts as a trustee of a trust, which holds shares in a client company, a self- interest and/or familiarity threat will arise. The threat to objectivity is potent where the shareholding is in excess of 5 per cent of the issued share capital of the company or of the total assets of the trust.*

(b) Where the trust holds shares in a company and the holding is in excess of 5 per cent of the issued share capital of the company, or the trust's aggregate investment in the company exceeds 5 per cent of the total assets comprised in the trust, the firm should not accept or continue appointment as auditors. The shareholdings (in relation to the issued share capital of the company) of trusts of which principals or members of staff of the firm are trustees should be regarded as aggregated for the purposes of this paragraph.

(c) The restrictions and aggregations contained in the preceding paragraph (b) above do not necessarily apply in the case of staff member trustees, where the trust is of a personal or family nature and is not client-related.

16.1.15 Safeguards in relation to trustee Holdings   (a) These include the following: (i) A trustee, or someone with whom a trustee is closely connected should not act as the principal or person responsible for the audit of the company in which the trustee is a shareholder.

(ii) A sole practitioner should not accept or continue appointment as an auditor of a trustee of a trust holding shares in that company unless he has made arrangements to consult externally with another member and that consultation confirms the propriety of accepting or continuing appointment.

(iii) The disclosure of the trust investment in the accounts, in the Directors' Report or in the Audit Report, save in the case of trustees shareholdings where the aggregate of all relevant shareholdings is less than one per cent of the issued capital of the company.

(iv) Where a close personal relationship develops in the course of a trustee shareholding, a member should have regard to the review procedures recommended in paragraphs 3.3.14 of chapter three (above).

(b) The above considerations apply where a person closely connected with the firm is a director or employee of a trust company, which acts as trustee of a trust holding investments in a company on the accounts of which the firm reports.

16.1.16 Area of risk - nominee shareholdings; 'bare trustee' shareholdings Similar considerations to those applying to trustee shareholdings (see above) apply also in the case of nominee shareholdings and 'bare trustee' shareholdings.

16.1.17 Area of risk - connections; associated firms; influences outside the practice employees

(a) It should be recognized that each of the threats dealt with in paragraphs 3.2.0. to 3.2.13. may arise either in relation to a principal of the firm, or in relation to a close connection such as a member of his immediate family (see paragraph 16.2.1 below). Threats can also arise because of pressures exerted upon a firm by an associated firm or an outside source introducing business, such as bankers, solicitors, or government.

(b) The threat to objectivity will depend upon the closeness of relationships and associations, the strength of an associate's interest in the firm retaining a client, and the

extent to which the introduction of business by an outside source is able to affect the firm's fee income.

(c) The audit firm should not employ any person on the audit who would by any of the foregoing principles be personally excluded from the role of auditor.

16.1.18 Safeguards in relation to connections etc.

(a) The possibility of a threat to objectivity arising in such circumstances should be borne in mind and provided for in the firm's review machinery. All the safeguards quoted in paragraphs 3.2.2 to 3.2.13 above are of potential relevance.   (b) It should be borne in mind that the threat to objectivity will be less where any connection is with a junior member of staff or with a member of the firm who is not personally engaged on the audit in question, and where his officer is distant from the office conducting the audit.

16.1.19 Area of risk - provision of other services to audit clients

(a) There are occasions where objectivity may be threatened or appear to be threatened by the provision to an audit client of services other than pure audit work. All the safeguards described in paragraphs 3.2.2 to 3.2.13 may have an application to the provision of other services.

(b) There is no objection to a firm providing advisory services to a company, which is additional to the audit. Care must be taken to ensure that the audit firm does not perform or be perceived to perform management functions or make management decisions. It is economic, in terms of skill and effort for Chartered Accountants in public practice to be able to provide other services to their clients since they already have a good knowledge of their business. Many companies (particularly smaller ones) would be adversely affected if they were denied the right to obtain other services from their auditors.

(c)   The threats that may arise in the course of providing other services are discussed   in the remainder of this chapter. The threats may be analyzed under the headings set out in paragraph 3.2.0 above.

16.2.0 The self - interest threat All work that creates a financial relationship between the auditor and the audit may appear to create a self-interest threat, as does payment for the audit itself. The nature of the threat sometimes perceived is that the auditor's objectivity might be impaired by a need to remain on good terms with the directors of the audited company in order to preserve a working relationship. The perceived threat grows with the size of the fees and is thus increased by work or services additional to the audit. But the most significant dimension of any threat, real or perceived, is likely to reside in the size of the total fees earned from a client in relation to the whole fees of the firm. This threat is addressed by the guidance on undue dependence in paragraph 16.1.1 to 16.1.2. above.

16.2.1 The self - review threat (a) Audit work itself gives rise to self-review. The auditor reviews matters that he has previously judged in prior year's audits, matters that were judged at planning stage, his recommendations (or lack of them) to management at previous audits, etc. In auditing, perhaps more than in any other activity, there is a need for a readiness to recognize and avoid past mistakes. The auditor must adopt the objectivity and independence of mind to be able to acknowledge past mistakes or errors of judgment and report fairly and afresh.

(b) The provision of other services may give rise to further needs for Self-review. If for example, the firm has designed or recommended any part of the systems or controls on which the audit relies, the audit team will need to take particular care to ensure that the audit judgments are objective, perhaps in the case of larger firms by arranging that there is little or no common membership between the systems work and the audit team.

(c) If, as is common for smaller companies, the auditor has prepared any of the data contained in the financial statements or drafted materials for the notes, or assisted in the preparation of the accounting records, a high degree of self-review threat arises.

(d) There is a spectrum of involvement by the auditor in the preparation of accounting records. It ranges from the situation prevailing in small companies where the auditor may prepare much of the accounting records and the financial statements as well as auditing whereas in the case of a major quoted company, the auditor does not participate in any part of the preparation process. Even in the latter case, the auditor who detects omissions in the company's proposed disclosures will normally suggest and draft the amendments required, so that in the end it is uncommon for a set of financial statements to appear where the auditor has had no hand whatsoever in the presentation or drafting.

(e) These processes of assistance, entailing self-review as they do, are not intrinsically damaging to audit objectivity, but pose a threat to it. Safeguards are necessary.

(f) At the smaller company end of the spectrum, the safeguards reside   in a considered analysis by the auditor of the work done in preparation of records and statements and careful consideration as to what separate audit procedures and scope are thus required. At the other end of the spectrum, in the case of a quoted company or other public interest company, an audit practice should not participate in the preparation of the company's accounts and accounting records save in relation to assistance of a routine clerical nature or in emergency. Such assistance might include, for example, work on the finalization of statutory accounts, including consolidations and tax provisions. The scale and nature of such work should be regularly reviewed.

16.2.2   Specialist valuations as an example of the self-review threat The provision to an audit client of specialist valuation services, which directly affect figures in the financial statements, gives rise to a clear self-review threat to objectivity.

A firm can audit a client's financial statements, which include the product of a specialist valuation carried out by it or an associated firm or organisation in the same country or overseas. Provided that such relationships, and competences of the personnel in the valuation of the key assignment are disclosed. Other safeguards taken by the auditor to reduce the self-review threat to an acceptable level must be documented. The steps include: (a) A careful consideration of the materiality of the amount involved in relation to the financial statement.   (b) Degree of subjectivity inherent in the items concerned.

(c) The reliability and extent of the identity base data.   The extent and clarity of related disclosures in a financial statement including the disclosures and as stated above, the identity of the provider of the expert services.

16.2.3

Advocacy threat

(a) Advocacy arises where a practitioner becomes an advocate for a client's position in any adversarial proceeding or situation. There is nothing improper about a position of advocacy and many types of professional services and support to a client may require it.

(b) Advocacy in a simple sense is always present when a firm supports its clients' interests. At the same time a professional person is always required to strive for objectivity in all professional work.

(c) But Advocacy can take a sharpened form, a more committed and protagonist form, where the firm supports its client in an adversarial situation.

(d)   An auditor's client is in principle the company and its shareholders. However his duty to that particular client must be set in the context of the wider public interest which requires him (through Companies and Allied Matters Act requirements and other relevant guidance and pronouncements) to provide an opinion as to whether a set of financial statements gives a "true and fair" view. That true and fair view must be an objective one, not tailored to or influenced by the needs of the client.

(e)   Hence advocacy in any sharpened form is likely to appear to the beholder to be incompatible with the particular objectivity required by the audit-reporting role. And in fact, particular advocacy roles, though adopted with objective judgement, may tend subsequently to form a degree of commitment in the professional's mind, which may make it difficult to return to the objectivity required for reporting.

(f)   The following examples are provided to illustrate the classes of professional services or other activity, which may give rise to these sharper forms of advocacy: (i) The recommendation, or promotion, of shares requires the adoption of a posture of advocacy in relation to the company concerned which cannot be compatible with objectivity in reporting. To recommend or promote shares usually requires a mental commitment to views or assertions about the strengths and qualities of the company. These views or assertions may have been reached by objective consideration, but once adopted the mental commitment does not readily permit a return to either the appearance or the reality of dispassionate and objective judgement.

(ii) By extension, leading a corporate finance team, which takes the responsibility for recommending or promoting shares, will be incompatible with objectivity in reporting. For this reason, there is a prohibition on the provision of such services to a company on which the firm reports.

(iii) The adoption of an extreme position on any issue of accounting principles, Taxation or other matter of professional judgments will always raise the risk of putting the practitioner into a position of sharpened advocacy. This will be heightened if it becomes necessary for the firm to support the extreme position in adversarial proceedings such as litigation or negotiations with government departments. Such a position may both raise doubts in the minds of observers and make it genuinely difficult for a firm to preserve its own audit objectivity on the topics at issue.

(g) The central issue for auditors in illustration (f) (iii) is the identification of what is or may become an extreme position. Members should endeavor to foresee such difficulties arising, and either avoid the extreme position or suggest to the company that it may seek alternate advisers to perform any role(s) requiring adversarial advocacy. It should be re-emphasized that there is nothing inherently unethical in advocating an extreme position on a client's behalf, if it can be supported by objective evidence. But it may be improper to perform such advocacy while at the same time asserting that the objectivity of the audit role has been maintained. In some situations, separation of roles between different partners may provide a degree of internal safeguards, but practitioners should recognize the risk of bringing themselves and the profession into disrepute by entering into a situation where a position of advocacy appears to indicate a position of commitment or a bias in state of mind which is not consistent with the objective state of mind required for a reporting role.

16.2.4 Involvement in management (a) Members are warned in particular of the dangers of being inadvertently drawn into the provision of management functions where a range of services has been provided to an audit client over a period of years. A member should be careful not to go beyond the advisory role and drift into the management sphere.

(b) The objections to an auditor becoming involved in a management role should be apparent. All of the threats to objectivity discussed above would affect the auditor who took management decisions, and their combined weight would make it virtually impossible for a member to claim to have retained objectivity in audit reporting. (c) A situation may arise where the practitioner tenders advice over a long period and the management of the company so frequently accepts and acts on the advice that it becomes difficult to separate the role of management from that of adviser. Members should ensure in every case that management accepts the judgments involved as its own after adequate consideration.

(d) A practitioner would need to consider the position carefully if the firm were invited to design systems affecting operations on which the commercial success of the company depended. It might even be desirable for management to consider taking an expert second opinion if the advice from the auditor and the ensuring management judgments were crucial to the company's financial and operational success. Many practitioners would judge that objectivity could be preserved in the audit only if management was well qualified with its own expertise to make all the operating judgments involved in the adoption and implementation of the system and if there were, among other internal safeguards, a considerable degree of separation of the system designers from the audit team.

(e) Recruitment of key financial and administrative staff for an audit client company is an instance where a firm should proceed with care. Whilst it is acceptable for the firm to advertise for and interview prospective staff and produce a 'short list' and recommendations, the final decision in every case as to whom to engage should be left to the client.

16.2.5 Area of risk - acting for a prolonged period of time Where the same engagement partner acts for an audit-client company for a prolonged period of time, a familiarity threat will arise.

16.2.6 The threat of over - familiarity (a) Professional relationships take time to develop, but once developed, they usually lead to maximum efficiency and effectiveness. Continuity of senior personnel on audit engagements is ordinarily to be encouraged both from the standpoint of the client and the Chartered Accountant in public practice. However, there is a concern that a long involvement by a single individual or audit team with an audit client could lead to the formulation of a close relationship which could be perceived to be a threat to objectivity and independence.

(b) Additionally, questions of quality control are affected, in that the Chartered Accountant with continued familiarity may over rely on that familiarity when carrying out audit procedures and making judgments on key decisions. The Chartered Accountant in public practice should therefore take steps to provide for an orderly rotation of senior personnel serving on the engagement. When rotation is impractical, review procedures should be designed to achieve the same objectives.

16.3.0 OTHER EXAMPLES OF SAFEGUARDS

16.3.1 Safeguards in relation to acting for prolonged period of time (a) Firms should, in relation to the audit of 'quoted companies' as defined in the definition section, ensure that no audit engagement partner remains in charge of such an audit for a period exceeding five (5) consecutive years. An audit engagement partner (see definition) who has ceased under the above provision to act as such should not return to that role in relation to that audit until a minimum of five years has passed, but is not precluded from other involvement with the client.

(b) A limited degree of flexibility over timing may be acceptable in circumstances where audit engagement partner continuity is especially important. Examples could include major changes to a company's structure or management, or its involvement in a take-over, which would otherwise coincide with the change of audit engagement partner.

(c) Because rotation of the audit engagement partner cannot be implemented by a sole- practitioner auditor, or by small firms where there is only one 'responsible individual', these should, in relation to the audit of quoted companies, be prepared to demonstrate that the following procedures have been carried out:

(i) Internal review at least annually, coupled with (ii) External consultation (see paragraph 16.4.1 (a)

16.4.0

Companies and clients other than those specified in 16.3.1 (i) The threat to a firm's objectivity arising from audit engagement partners continuing in such roles for a prolonged period remains in relation to all clients and not merely those specified in paragraph 16.3.1 the same considerations apply in respect of senior audit staff. Members, should therefore, establish adequate review machinery along the lines indicated in paragraphs 16.3.1 (a)(b)(c) above, including an annual review, in order to satisfy themselves that each engagement may properly be accepted or continued.

16.4.1 Comments: Sole Practitioners and small firms;

(a) Not all the safeguards suggested in the course of the preceding guidance will be available to the sole practitioners within his firm. The practitioners should therefore set up alternative standing arrangements to consult externally with another member. Arrangements with another practitioner could include the provisions by the latter of the client's confidentiality and an undertaking not to accept instructions from any client whose work is the subject of review for a period of two years thereafter.

The involvement of a third party such as a clients audit committee, or regulatory body or another firm is a form of safeguard.

(b) Where the practitioner's own review indicates that an audit engagement should only be accepted or continued with additional safeguards to protect the practitioner's independence, he should undertake such consultation before proceeding further. The extent of the consultation will vary according to the nature of the problem; in some cases it may be confined to a discussion of principles; in others it may involve an examination of the file or a discussion of personal relationships.

(C) Refusal to act where no other course can abate the perceived problem: Some exclusions and prohibitions are the subject of statute or regulation outside the control of the profession. In addition, there are some situations in which the threat to an auditor's objectivity is so significant, or generally perceived to be so, that an auditor should, having regard to preservation of the public image of his profession, decline to accept appointment, even if he believes that the circumstances are such that available safeguards and procedures could, in his particular case, enable him to maintain proper objectivity. In this eventuality, he should decline or resign appointment.

(d) It follows from the preceding paragraphs that the perception of the public (or any section of it) that an auditor's objectivity may be threatened is not, of itself, a reason why an appointment should be refused. The countervailing pressures and safeguards described above may often override a threat. Members and firms are encouraged to make clients and others outside the profession aware of the compliance procedures that they employ.

CHAPTER SEVENTEEN
17.1.0 APPLICATION OF FRAMEWORK TO SPECIFIC SITUATIONS
17.1.1   Introduction
The following examples describe specific circumstances and relationships that may create threats to independence. The examples describe the potential threats created and the safeguards that may be appropriate to eliminate the threats or reduce them to an acceptable level in each circumstance. The examples are not all inclusive. In practice, the firm, network firms and the members of the assurance team will be required to assess the implications of similar, but different, circumstances and relationships and to determine whether safeguards, including the safeguards in chapters 3 and 16 can be applied to satisfactorily address the threats to independence.

17.1.2 Some of the examples deal with financial statement audit clients while others deal with assurance engagements for clients that are not financial statement audit clients. They illustrate how safeguards should be applied to fulfill the requirement for the members of the assurance team, the firm and network firms to be independent of a financial statement audit client, and for the members of the assurance team and the firm to be independent of an assurance client that is not a financial statement audit client.

17.1.3 The examples do not include assurance reports to a non-financial statement audit client expressly restricted for use by identified users. For such engagements, members of the assurance team and their immediate and close family are required to be independent of the assurance client. Further, the firm should not have a material financial interest, direct or indirect, in the assurance client.

17.1.4 The examples illustrate how the framework applies to financial statement audit clients and other assurance clients. The examples should be read in conjunction with chapter 15.0.0, which explain that, in the majority of assurance engagements, there is one responsible party and that responsible party comprises the assurance client. However, in some assurance engagements there are two responsible parties. In such circumstances, consideration should be given to any threats the firm has reason to believe may be created by interests and relationships between a member of the assurance team, the firm, a network firm and the party responsible for the subject matter.

17.2.0 Financial Interests

17.2.1 A financial interest in an assurance client may create a self-interest threat. In evaluating the significance of the threat, and the appropriate safeguards to be applied to eliminate the threat or reduce it to an acceptable level, it is necessary to examine the nature of the financial interest. This includes an evaluation of the role of the person holding the financial interest, the materiality of the financial interest and the type of financial interest (direct or indirect).

17.2.2 When evaluating the type of financial interest, consideration should be given to the fact that financial interests range from those where the individual has no control over the investment vehicle or the financial interest held (e.g., a mutual fund, unit trust or similar intermediary vehicle) to those where the individual has control over the financial interest (e.g., as a trustee) or is able to influence investment decisions. In evaluating the significance of any threat to independence, it is important to consider the degree of control or influence that can be exercised over the intermediary, the financial interest held, or its investment strategy. When control exists, the financial interest should be considered direct. Conversely, when the holder of the financial interest has no ability to exercise such control the financial interest should be considered indirect.

17.3.0 Provisions Applicable to All Assurance Clients

17.3.1 If a member of the assurance team, or their immediate family member, has a direct financial interest or a material indirect financial interest, in the assurance client, the self- interest threat created would be so significant the only safeguards available to eliminate the threat or reduce it to an acceptable level would be to:

(a) Dispose of the direct financial interest prior to the individual becoming a member of the assurance team;   (b)   Dispose of the indirect financial interest in total or dispose of a sufficient   amount of it so that the remaining interest is no longer material prior to the individual becoming a member of the assurance team; or

(C)   Remove the member of the assurance team from the assurance engagement.

17.3.2 If a member of the assurance team, or their immediate family member receives, by way of, for example, an inheritance, gift or, as a result of a merger, a direct financial interest or a material indirect financial interest in the assurance client, a self-interest threat would be created. The following safeguards should be applied to eliminate the threat or reduce it to an acceptable level:

(a) Disposing of the financial interest at the earliest practical date; or   (b) Removing the member of the assurance team from the assurance engagement. During the period prior to disposal of the financial interest or the removal of the individual from the assurance team, consideration should be given to whether additional safeguards are necessary to reduce the threat to an acceptable level. Such safeguards might include: (i) Discussing the matter with those charged with governance, such as the audit committee; or   (ii) Involving an additional Chartered Accountant to review the work   done, or otherwise advise as necessary.

17.3.3 When a member of the assurance team knows that his or her close family member has a direct financial interest or a material indirect financial interest in the assurance client, a self-interest threat may be created. In evaluating the significance of any threat, consideration should be given to the nature of the relationship between the member of the assurance team and the close family member and the materiality of the financial interest. Once the significance of the threat has been evaluated, safeguards should be considered and applied as necessary. Such safeguards might include:

(a) The close family member disposing of all or a sufficient portion of the financial interest at the earliest practical date;

(b) Discussing the matter with those charged with governance, such as the audit committee;

(c) Involving an additional Chartered Accountant who did not take part in the assurance engagement to review the work done by the member of the assurance team with the close family relationship or otherwise advise as necessary; or

(d) Removing the individual from the assurance engagement.   17.3.4 When a firm or a member of the assurance team holds a direct financial interest or a material indirect financial interest in the assurance client as a trustee, a self-interest threat may be created by the possible influence of the trust over the assurance client. Accordingly, such an interest should only be held when:

(a)   The member of the assurance team, an immediate family member of the member of the assurance team, and the firm are not beneficiaries of the trust;

(b)   The interest held by the trust in the assurance client is not material to the trust;   (c)   The trust is not able to exercise significant influence over the assurance client; and   (d) The member of the assurance team or the firm does not have significant influence over any investment decision involving a financial interest in the assurance client.   17.3.5 Consideration should be given to whether a self-interest threat may be created by the financial interests of individuals outside of the assurance team and their immediate and close family members. Such individuals would include: (a)   Partners, and their immediate family members, who are not members of the assurance team;

(b)   Partners and managerial employees who provide non-assurance services to the assurance client; and

(c)   Individuals who have a close personal relationship with a member of the assurance team. Whether the interests held by such individuals may create a self-interest threat will depend upon factors such as:

(d) The firm's organizational, operating and reporting structure; and   (e) The nature of the relationship between the individual and the member of the assurance team. 17.3.6   The significance of the threat should be evaluated and, if the threat is other than clearly insignificant, safeguards should be considered and applied as necessary to reduce the threat to an acceptable level. Such safeguards might include:

(a)   Put in place appropriate, policies to restrict people from holding such interests;

(b) Discussing the matter with those charged with governance, such as the audit committee; or

(c) Involving an additional Chartered Accountant who did not take part in the assurance engagement to review the work done or otherwise advise as necessary.

17.3.7 When an inadvertent violation of this section as it relates to a financial interest in an assurance client would not impair the independence of the firm, the network firm or a member of the assurance team when:

(a)   The firm, and the network firm, have established policies and procedures that require all professionals to report promptly to the firm any breaches resulting from the purchase, inheritance or other acquisition of a financial interest in the assurance client;

(b)   The firm, and the network firm, promptly notify the professional that the financial interest should be disposed of; and

(b) The disposal occurs at the earliest practical date after identification of the issue, or the professional is removed from the assurance team.

17.3.8 When an inadvertent violation of this section relating to a financial interest in an   assurance client has occurred, the firm should consider whether any safeguards should be applied. Such safeguards might include: (a) Involving an additional Chartered Accountant who did not take part in the assurance   engagement to review the work done by the member of the assurance team; or (b) Excluding the individual from any substantive decision-making concerning the assurance engagement.

17.4.0 Provisions Applicable to Financial Statement Audit Clients.   17.4.1 If a firm, or a network firm, has a direct financial interest in a financial statement audit client of the firm the self-interest threat created would be so significant no safeguard could reduce the threat to an acceptable level. Consequently, disposal of the financial interest would be the only action appropriate to permit the firm to perform the engagement.

17.4.2 If a firm, or a network firm, has a material indirect financial interest in a financial statement audit client of the firm, a self-interest threat is also created. The only actions appropriate to permit the firm to perform the engagement would be for the firm, or the network firm, either to dispose of the indirect interest in total or to dispose of a sufficient amount of it so that the remaining interest is no longer material.

17.4.3 If a firm, or a network firm, has a material financial interest in an entity that has a controlling interest in a financial statement audit client, the self-interest threat created would be so significant no safeguard could reduce the threat to an acceptable level. The only actions appropriate to permit the firm to perform the engagement would be for the firm, or the network firm, either to dispose of the financial interest in total or to dispose of a sufficient amount of it so that the remaining interest is no longer material.

17.4.4 If the retirement benefits plan of a firm, or network firm, has a financial interest in a financial statement audit client, a self-interest threat may be created. Accordingly, the significance of any such threat created should be evaluated and, if the threat is other than clearly insignificant, safeguards should be considered and applied as necessary to eliminate the threat or reduce it to an acceptable level. 17.4.5 If other partners, including partners who do not perform assurance engagements, or their immediate family, in the office` in which the engagement partner practices in connection with the financial statement audit hold a direct financial interest or a material indirect financial interest in that audit client, the self-interest threat created would be so significant no safeguard could reduce the threat to an acceptable level. Accordingly, such partners or their immediate family should not hold any such financial interests in such an audit client.

17.4.6 The office in which the engagement partner practices in connection with the financial statement audit is not necessarily the office to which that partner is assigned. Accordingly, when the engagement partner is located in a different office from that of the other members of the assurance team, judgment should be used to determine in which office the partner practices in connection with that audit.

17.4.7 If other partners and managerial employees who provide non-assurance services to the financial statement audit client, except those whose involvement is clearly insignificant, or their immediate family, hold a direct financial interest or a material indirect financial interest in the audit client, the self-interest threat created would be so significant no safeguard could reduce the threat to an acceptable level. Accordingly, such personnel or their immediate family should not hold any such financial interests in such an audit client.

17.4.8 A financial interest in a financial statement audit client that is held by an immediate family member of (a) a partner located in the office in which the engagement partner practices in connection with the audit, or (b) a partner or managerial employee who provides non-assurance services to the audit client is not considered to create an unacceptable threat provided it is received as a result of their employment rights (e.g.,

Pension rights or share options) and, where necessary, appropriate safeguards are applied to reduce any threat to independence to an acceptable level.

17.4.9 A self-interest threat may be created if the firm, or the network firm, or a member of the assurance team has an interest in an entity and a financial statement audit client, or a director, officer or controlling owner thereof also has an investment in that entity. Independence is not compromised with respect to the audit client if the respective interests of the firm, the network firm, or member of the assurance team, and the audit client, or director, officer or controlling owner thereof are both immaterial and the audit client cannot exercise significant influence over the entity. If an interest is material, to the firm, the network firm or the audit client, and the audit client can exercise significant influence over the entity, no safeguards are available to reduce the threat to an acceptable level and the firm, or the network firm, should either dispose of the interest or decline the audit engagement. Any member of the assurance team with such a material interest should either:

(a) Dispose of the interest;   (b) Dispose of a sufficient amount of the interest so that the remaining interest is no longer material; or (c) Withdraw from the audit.

17.5.0 Provisions Applicable to Non-Financial Statement Audit Assurance Clients.

17.5.1 If a firm has a direct financial interest in an assurance client that is not a financial statement audit client the self-interest threat created would be so significant no safeguard could reduce the threat to an acceptable level. Consequently, disposal of the financial interest would be the only action appropriate to permit the firm to perform the engagement.

17.5.2 If a firm has a material indirect financial interest in an assurance client that is not a financial statement audit client a self-interest threat is also created. The only action appropriate to permit the firm to perform the engagement would be for the firm to either dispose of the indirect interest in total or to dispose of a sufficient amount of it so that the remaining interest is no longer material.

17.53 If a firm has a material financial interest in an entity that has a controlling interest in an assurance client that is not a financial statement audit client, the self-interest threat created would be so significant no safeguard could reduce the threat to an acceptable level. The only action appropriate to permit the firm to perform the engagement would be for the firm either to dispose of the financial interest in total or to dispose of a sufficient amount of it so that the remaining interest is no longer material.

17.5.4 When a restricted use report for an assurance engagement that is not a financial statement audit engagement is issued, exceptions to the provisions in paragraphs 18.3.0 through 18.3.4, 18.3.6 through 18.5.2 are set out in paragraph 14.1.0 of chapter fourteen.

17.6.0 Loans and Guarantees   17.6.1 A loan, or a guarantee of a loan, to the firm from an assurance client that is a bank or a similar institution, would not create a threat to independence provided the loan, or guarantee, is made under normal lending procedures, terms and requirements and the loan is immaterial to both the firm and the assurance client. If the loan is material to the assurance client or the firm it may be possible, *through the application of safeguards, to reduce the self-interest threat created to an acceptable level. Such safeguards might include involving an additional Chartered Accountant from outside the firm, or network firm, to review the work performed.*

17.6.2 A loan, or a guarantee of a loan, from an assurance client that is a bank or a similar institution, to a member of the assurance team or their immediate family would not create a threat to independence provided the loan, or guarantee, is made under normal lending procedures, terms and requirements. Examples of such loans include home mortgages, bank overdrafts, car loans and credit card balances.

17.6.3 Similarly, deposits made by, or brokerage accounts of, a firm or a member of the assurance team with an assurance client that is a bank, broker or similar institution would not create a threat to independence provided the deposit or account is held under normal commercial terms.

17.6.4 If the firm, or a member of the assurance team, makes a loan to an assurance client, that is not a bank or similar institution, or guarantees such an assurance client's borrowing, the self-interest threat created would be so significant no safeguard could reduce the threat to an acceptable level, unless the loan or guarantee is immaterial to both the firm or the member of the assurance team and the assurance client.

17.6.5 Similarly, if the firm or a member of the assurance team accepts a loan from, or has borrowing guaranteed by, an assurance client that is not a bank or similar institution, the self-interest threat created would be so significant no safeguard could reduce the threat to an acceptable level, unless the loan or guarantee is immaterial to both the firm or the member of the assurance team and the assurance client.

17.6.6 The examples in paragraphs 18.6.1 through 18.6.5 relate to loans and guarantees between the firm and an assurance client. In the case of a financial statement audit engagement, the provisions should be applied to the firm; all network firms and the audit client.

17.7.0 Close Business Relationships with Assurance Clients

17.7.1 A close business relationship between a firm or a member of the assurance team and the assurance client or its management, or between the firm, a network firm and a financial statement audit client, will involve a commercial or common financial interest and may create self-interest and intimidation threats. The following are examples of such relationships:

(a) Having a material financial interest in a joint venture with the assurance client or a controlling owner, director, officer or other individual who performs senior managerial functions for that client.

(b) Arrangements to combine one or more services or products of the firm with one or more services or products of the assurance client and to market the package with reference to both parties.

(c) Distribution or marketing arrangements under which the firm acts as a distributor or marketer of the assurance client's products or services, or the assurance client acts as the distributor or marketer of the products or services of the firm.

17.7.2 In the case of a financial statement audit client, unless the financial interest is immaterial and the relationship is clearly insignificant to the firm, the network firm and the audit client, no safeguards could reduce the threat to an acceptable level.

17.7.3 In the case of an assurance client that is not a financial statement audit client, unless the financial interest is immaterial and the relationship is clearly insignificant to the firm and the assurance client, no safeguards could reduce the threat to an acceptable level. Consequently, in both these circumstances the only possible courses of action are to:

(a) Terminate the business relationship;

(b) Reduce the magnitude of the relationship so that the financial interest is immaterial and the relationship is clearly insignificant; or

(c) Refuse to perform the assurance engagement. Unless any such financial interest is immaterial and the relationship is clearly insignificant to the member of the assurance team, the only appropriate safeguard would be to remove the individual from the assurance team.

17.7.4 In the case of a financial statement audit client, business relationships involving an interest held by the firm, a network firm or a member of the assurance team or their immediate family in a closely held entity when the audit client or a director or officer of the audit client, or any group thereof, also has an interest in that entity, do not create threats to independence provided: (a) The relationship is clearly insignificant to the firm, the network firm and the audit client; (b) The interest held is immaterial to the investor, or group of investors; and (c) The interest does not give the investor, or group of investors, the ability to control the closely held entity.

17.7.5 The purchase of goods and services from an assurance client by the firm (or from a financial statement audit client by a network firm) or a member of the assurance team would not generally create a threat to independence providing the transaction is in the normal course of business and on an arm's length basis. However, such transactions may be of a nature or magnitude so as to create a self-interest threat. If the threat created is other than clearly insignificant, safeguards should be considered and applied as necessary to reduce the threat to an acceptable level. Such safeguards might include:

(a) Eliminating or reducing the magnitude of the transaction; (b) Removing the individual from the assurance team; or (c) Discussing the issue with those charged with governance, such as the audit committee.

17.8.0 Family and Personal Relationships

17.8.1 Family and personal relationships between a member of the assurance team and a director, an officer or certain employees, depending on their role, of the assurance client, may create self-interest, familiarity or intimidation threats. It is impracticable to attempt to describe in detail the significance of the threats that such relationships may create. The significance will depend upon a number of factors including the individual's responsibilities on the assurance engagement, the closeness of the relationship and the role of the family member or other individual within the assurance client. Consequently, there is a wide spectrum of circumstances that will need to be evaluated and safeguards to be applied to reduce the threat to an acceptable level.

17.8.2 When an immediate family member of a member of the assurance team is a director, an officer or an employee of the assurance client in a position to exert direct and significant influence over the subject matter information of the assurance engagement, or was in such a position during any period covered by the engagement, the threats to independence can only be reduced to an acceptable level by removing the individual from the assurance team. The closeness of the relationship is such that no other safeguard could reduce the threat to independence to an acceptable level. If application of this safeguard is not used, the only course of action is to withdraw from the assurance engagement. For example, in the case of an audit of financial statements, if the spouse of a member of the assurance team is an employee in a position to exert direct and significant influence over the preparation of the audit client's accounting records or financial statements, the threat to independence could only be reduced to an acceptable level by removing the individual from the assurance team.

17.8.3 When an immediate family member of a member the assurance team is an employee in a position to exert direct and significant influence over the subject matter of the engagement, threats to independence may be created. The significance of the threats will depend on factors such as:

(a) The position the immediate family member holds with the client; and (b) The role of the professional on the assurance team.

The significance of the threat should be evaluated and, if the threat is other than clearly insignificant, safeguards should be considered and applied as necessary to reduce the threat to an acceptable level. Such safeguards might include:

(i) Removing the individual from the assurance team; Where possible, structuring the responsibilities of the assurance team so that the professional does not deal with matters that are within the responsibility of the immediate family member; or

(ii) Policies and procedures to empower staff to communicate to senior levels within the firm any issue of independence and objectivity that concerns them.

17.8.4 When a close family member of a member of the assurance team is a director, an officer, or an employee of the assurance client in a position to exert direct and significant influence over the subject matter information of the assurance engagement, threats to independence may be created. The significance of the threats will depend on factors such as:

(a) The position the close family member holds with the client; and (b) Role of the professional on the assurance team.

17.8.5 The significance of the threat should be evaluated and, if the threat is other than clearly insignificant, safeguards should be considered and applied as necessary to reduce the threat to an acceptable level. Such safeguards might include:

(a) Removing the individual from the assurance team; (b) Where possible, structuring the responsibilities of the assurance team so that the professional does not deal with matters that are within the responsibility of the close family member; or (c) Policies and procedures to empower staff to communicate to senior levels within the firm any issue of independence and objectivity that concerns them. 17.8.6 In addition, self-interest,

familiarity or intimidation threats may be created when a person who is other than an immediate or close family member of a member of the assurance team has a close relationship with the member of the assurance team and is a director, an officer or an employee of the assurance client in a position to exert direct and significant influence over the subject matter information of the assurance engagement. Therefore, members of the assurance team are responsible for identifying any such persons and for consulting in accordance with firm procedures. The evaluation of the significance of any threat created and the safeguards appropriate to eliminate the threat or reduce it to an acceptable level will include considering matters such as the closeness of the relationship and the role of the individual within the assurance client.

17.8.7 Consideration should be given to whether self-interest, familiarity or intimidation threats may be created by a personal or family relationship between a partner or employee of the firm who is not a member of the assurance team and a director, an officer or an employee of the assurance client in a position to exert direct and significant influence over the subject matter information of the assurance engagement. Therefore partners and employees of the firm are responsible for identifying any such relationships and for consulting in accordance with firm procedures. The evaluation of the significance of any threat created and the safeguards appropriate to eliminate the threat or reduce it to an acceptable level will include considering matters such as the closeness of the relationship, the interaction of the firm professional with the assurance team, the position held within the firm, and the role of the individual within the assurance client.

17.8.8 An inadvertent violation of this section as it relates to family and personal relationships would not impair the independence of a firm or a member of the assurance team when:

(a) The firm has established policies and procedures that require all professionals to report promptly to the firm any breaches resulting from changes in the employment status of their immediate or close family members or other personal relationships that create threats to independence;

(b) Either the responsibilities of the assurance team are re-structured so that the professional does not deal with matters that are within the responsibility of the person with whom he or she is related or has a personal relationship, or, if this is not possible, the firm promptly removes the professional from the assurance engagement; and

(c) Additional care is given to reviewing the work of the professional.

17.8.9 When an inadvertent violation of this section relating to family and personal relationships has occurred, the firm should consider whether any safeguards should be applied. Such safeguards might include:

(a) Involving an additional professional accountant who did not take part in the assurance engagement to review the work done by the member of the assurance team; or

(b) Excluding the individual from any substantive decision-making concerning the assurance engagement.

17.9.0 Employment with Assurance Clients

17.9.1 A firm or a member of the assurance team's independence may be threatened if a director, an officer or an employee of the assurance client in a position to exert direct and significant influence over the subject matter information of the assurance engagement has been a member of the assurance team or partner of the firm. Such circumstances may create self-interest, familiarity and intimidation threats particularly when significant connections remain between the individual and his or her former firm. Similarly, a member of the assurance team's independence may be threatened when an individual participates in the assurance engagement knowing, or having reason to believe, that he or she is to, or may, join the assurance client some time in the future.

17.9.2 If a member of the assurance team, partner or former partner of the firm has joined the assurance client, the significance of the self-interest, familiarity or intimidation threats created will depend upon the following factors:

(a)   The position the individual has taken at the assurance client.   (b)   The amount of any involvement the individual will have with the assurance team. (c)   The length of time that has passed since the individual was a member of the assurance team or firm.   (d)   The former position of the individual within the assurance team or firm.

17.9.3 The significance of the threat should be evaluated and, if the threat is other than clearly insignificant, safeguards should be considered and applied as necessary to reduce the threat to an acceptable level. Such safeguards might include:

(a) Considering the appropriateness or necessity of modifying the assurance plan for the assurance engagement;   (b)   Assigning an assurance team to the subsequent assurance engagement that is of sufficient experience in relation to the individual who has joined the assurance client; (c)   Involving an additional professional accountant who was not a member of the assurance team to review the work done or otherwise advise as necessary; or

(d) Quality control review of the assurance engagement. In all cases, all of the following safeguards are necessary to reduce the threat to an acceptable level:

(i)   the individual concerned is not entitled to any benefits or payments from the firm unless these are made in accordance with fixed pre-determined   arrangements. In addition, any amount owed to the individual should not be of such significance to threaten the firm's independence.

(ii) the individual does not continue to participate or appear to participate in the firm's business or professional activities.

17.9.4   A self-interest threat is created when a member of the assurance team participates in the assurance engagement while knowing, or having reason to believe, that he or she is to, or may, join the assurance client some time in the future. This threat can be reduced to an acceptable level by the application of all of the following safeguards:

(a) Policies and procedures to require the individual to notify the firm when entering serious employment negotiations with the assurance client.   (b) Removal of the individual from the assurance engagement. In addition, consideration should be given to performing an independent review of any significant judgments made by that individual while on the engagement.

17.10.0 Recent Service with Assurance Clients.

17.10.1 To have a former officer, director or employee of the assurance client serve as a member of the assurance team may create self-interest, self-review and familiarity threats. This would be particularly true when a member of the assurance team has to report on, for example, subject matter information he or she had prepared or elements of the financial statements he or she had valued while with the assurance client. 17.10.2 If, during the period covered by the assurance report, a member of the assurance team had served as an officer or director of the assurance client, or had been an employee in a position to exert direct and significant influence over the subject matter information of the assurance engagement, the threat created would be so significant no safeguard Could reduce the threat to an acceptable level. Consequently, such individuals should not be assigned to the assurance team.

17.10.3 If, prior to the period covered by the assurance report, a member of the assurance team had served as an officer or director of the assurance client, or had been an employee in a position to exert direct and significant influence over the subject matter information of the assurance engagement, this may create self-interest, self-review and familiarity threats. For example, such threats would be created if a decision made or work performed by the individual in the prior period, while employed by the assurance client, is to be evaluated in the current period as part of the current assurance engagement. The significance of the threats will depend upon factors such as: (a) The position the individual held with the assurance client;

(b) The length of time that has passed since the individual left the assurance client; and

(c) The role the individual plays on the assurance team. The significance of the threat should be evaluated and, if the threat is other than clearly insignificant, safeguards should be considered and applied as necessary to reduce the threat to an acceptable level. Such safeguards might include:

(d) Involving an additional professional accountant to review the work done by the individual as part of the assurance team or otherwise advise as necessary; or

(e) Discussing the issue with those charged with governance, such as the audit committee.

17.11.0 Serving as an Officer or Director on the Board of Assurance Clients

17.11.1 If a partner or employee of the firm serves as an officer or as a director on the board of an assurance client the self-review and self-interest threats created would be so significant no safeguard could reduce the threats to an acceptable level. In the case of a financial statement audit engagement, if a partner or employee of a network firm were to serve as an officer or as a director on the board of the audit client the threats created would be so significant no safeguard could reduce the threats to an acceptable level. Consequently, if such an individual were to accept such a position the only course of action is to refuse to perform, or to withdraw from the assurance engagement.

17.11.2 The position of Company Secretary has different implications in different jurisdictions. The duties may range from administrative duties such as personnel management and the maintenance of company records and registers, to duties as diverse as ensuring that the company complies with regulations or providing advice on corporate governance matters. Generally this position is seen to imply a close degree of association with the entity and may create self-review and advocacy threats.

17.11.3   If a partner or employee of the firm or a network firm serves as Company Secretary for a financial statement audit client the self-review and advocacy threats created would generally be so significant, no safeguard could reduce the threat to an acceptable level. When the practice is specifically permitted under local law, professional rules or practice, the duties and functions undertaken should be limited to those of a routine and formal administrative nature such as the preparation of minutes and maintenance of statutory returns.

17.11.4   Routine administrative services to support a company secretarial function or advisory work in relation to company secretarial administration matters is generally not perceived to impair independence, provided client management makes all relevant decisions.

17.12.0 Long Association of Senior Personnel with Assurance Clients

General Provisions 17.12.1 Using the same senior personnel on an assurance engagement over a long period of time may create a familiarity threat. The significance of the threat will depend upon factors such as:

(a) The length of time that the individual has been a member of the assurance team;   (b) The role of the individual on the assurance team;   (c) The structure of the firm; and   (d) The nature of the assurance engagement.

The significance of the threat should be evaluated and, if the threat is other than clearly insignificant, safeguards should be considered and applied to reduce the threat to an acceptable level. Such safeguards might include:

(i) Rotating the senior personnel off the assurance team;   (ii) Involving an additional professional accountant who was not a member of the assurance team to review the work done by the senior personnel or otherwise advise as necessary; or (iii) Independent internal quality reviews.

17.13.0 Financial Statement Audit Clients That are Listed Entities

17.13.1 Using the same engagement partner or the same individual responsible for the engagement quality control review on a financial statement audit over a prolonged period may create a familiarity threat. This threat is particularly relevant in the context of the financial statement audit of a listed entity and safeguards should be applied in such situations to reduce such threat to an acceptable level. Accordingly in respect of the financial statement audit of listed entities:

(a) The engagement partner and the individual responsible for the engagement quality control review should be rotated after serving in either capacity, or a combination thereof, for a pre-defined period, normally no more than 5 years and

(b) Such an individual rotating after a pre-defined period should not participate in the audit engagement until a further period of time, normally two years, has elapsed.

17.13.2 When a financial statement audit client becomes a listed entity the length of time the engagement partner or the individual responsible for the engagement quality control review has served the audit client in that capacity should be considered in determining when the individual should be rotated. However, the person may continue to serve as the engagement partner or as the individual responsible for the engagement quality control review for two additional years before rotating off the engagement.

17.13.3 While the engagement partner and the individual responsible for the engagement quality control review should be rotated after such a pre-defined period, some degree of flexibility over timing of rotation may be necessary in certain circumstances. Examples of such circumstances include: (a) Situations when the person's continuity is especially important to the financial statement audit client, for example, when there will be major changes to the audit client's structure that would otherwise coincide with the rotation of the person's; and   (b) Situations when, due to the size of the firm, rotation is not possible or does not constitute an appropriate safeguard. In all such circumstances when the person is not rotated after such a pre-defined period, equivalent safeguards should be applied to reduce any threats to an acceptable level.

17.13.4 When a firm has only a few people with the necessary knowledge and experience to serve as engagement partner or individual responsible for the engagement quality control review on a financial statement audit client that is a listed entity, rotation may not be an appropriate safeguard. In these circumstances the firm should apply other safeguards to reduce the threat to an acceptable level. Such safeguards would include involving an additional professional accountant who was not otherwise associated with the assurance team to review the work done or otherwise advise as necessary. This individual could be someone from outside the firm or someone within the firm who was not otherwise associated with the assurance team

17.14.0   Provision of Non-assurance Services to Assurance Clients.

17.14.1 Firms have traditionally provided to their assurance clients a range of non- assurance services that are consistent with their skills and expertise. Assurance client's value the benefits that derive from having these firms, which have a good understanding of the business, bring their knowledge and skill to bear in other areas. Furthermore, the provision of such non-assurance services will often result in the assurance team obtaining information regarding the assurance client's business and operations that is helpful in relation to the assurance engagement. The greater the knowledge of the assurance client's business, the better the assurance team will understand the assurance client's procedures and controls, and the business and financial risks that it faces. The provision of non-assurance services may, however, create threats to the independence of the firm, a network firm or the members of the assurance team, particularly with respect to perceived threats to independence. Consequently, it is necessary to evaluate the significance of any threat created by the provision of such services. In some cases it may be possible to eliminate or reduce the threat created by application of safeguards. In other cases no safeguards are available to reduce the threat to an acceptable   level.

17.14.2 The following activities would generally create self-interest or self-review threats that are so significant that only avoidance of the activity or refusal to perform the assurance engagement would reduce the threats to an acceptable level:

(a) Exercising authority on behalf of the assurance client, or having the authority to do so. (b) Determining which recommendation of the firm should be implemented. (c) Reporting, in a management role, to those charged with governance

17.14.3 The examples set out in paragraphs 18.1.0. through 18.14.3 are addressed in the context of the provision of non-assurance services to an assurance client. The potential threats to independence will most frequently arise when a non-assurance service is provided to a financial statement audit client. The financial statements of an entity provide financial information about a broad range of transactions and events that have affected the entity. The subject matter information of other assurance services, however, may be limited in nature. Threats to independence, however, may also arise when a firm provides a non-assurance service related to the subject matter information, of a nonfinancial statement audit assurance engagement. In such cases, consideration should be given to the significance of the firm's involvement with the subject matter information, of the engagement, whether any self-review threats are created and whether any threats to independence could be reduced to an acceptable level by application of safeguards, or whether the engagement should be declined. When the non-assurance service is not related to the subject matter information, of the non-financial statement audit assurance engagement, the threats to independence will generally be clearly insignificant.

17.14.4 The following activities may also create self-review or self-interest threats: (a) Having custody of an assurance client's assets.

(b) Supervising assurance client employees in the performance of their normal recurring activities. (c) Preparing source documents or originating data, in electronic or other form, evidencing the occurrence of a transaction (for example, purchase orders, payroll time records, and customer orders).

The significance of any threat created should be evaluated and, if the threat is other than clearly insignificant, safeguards should be considered and applied as necessary to eliminate the threat or reduce it to an acceptable level. Such safeguards might include:

(a) Making arrangements so that personnel providing such services do not participate in the assurance engagement;

(b) Involving an additional Chartered Accountant to advise on the potential impact of the activities on the independence of the firm and the assurance team; or (c) Other relevant safeguards set out in national regulations and relevant laws

17.14.5 New developments in business, the evolution of financial markets, rapid changes in information technology, and the consequences for management and control, make it impossible to draw up an all-inclusive list of all situations when providing non-assurance services to an assurance client might create threats to independence and of the different safeguards that might eliminate these threats or reduce them to an acceptable level. In general, however, a firm may provide services beyond the assurance engagement provided any threats to independence have been reduced to an acceptable level.

17.14.6 The following safeguards may be particularly relevant in reducing to an acceptable level threats created by the provision of non-assurance services to assurance clients:

(a) Policies and procedures to prohibit professional staff from making management decisions for the assurance client, or assuming responsibility for such decisions.

(b) Discussing independence issues related to the provision of non-assurance services with those charged with governance, such as the audit committee.

(c) Policies within the assurance client regarding the oversight responsibility for provision of non-assurance services by the firm.

(d) Involving an additional professional accountant to advise on the potential impact of the non-assurance engagement on the independence of the member of the assurance team and the firm.

(e) Involving an additional professional accountant outside of the firm to provide assurance on a discrete aspect of the assurance engagement.

(f) Obtaining the assurance client's acknowledgement of responsibility for the results of the work performed by the firm.

(g) Disclosing to those charged with governance, such as the audit committee, the nature and extent of fees charged.

(h) Making arrangements so that personnel providing non-assurance services do not participate in the assurance engagement.

17.14.7 Before the firm accepts an engagement to provide a non-assurance service to an assurance client, consideration should be given to whether the provision of such a service would create a threat to independence. In situations when a threat created is other than clearly insignificant, the non-assurance engagement should be declined unless appropriate safeguards can be applied to eliminate the threat or reduce it to an acceptable level. 17.14.8 The provision of certain non-assurance services to financial statement audit clients may create threats to independence so significant that no safeguard could eliminate the threat or reduce it to an acceptable level. However, the provision of such services to a related entity, division or discrete financial statement item of such clients may be permissible when any threats to the firm's independence have been reduced to an acceptable level by arrangements for that related entity, division or discrete financial statement item to be audited by another firm or when another firm re-performs the non-assurance service to the extent necessary to enable it to take responsibility for that service.

17.15.0 Preparing Accounting Records and Financial Statements.

17.15.1 Assisting a financial statement audit client in matters such as preparing accounting records or financial statements may create a self-review threat when the firm subsequently audits the financial statements.

17.15.2 It is the responsibility of financial statement audit client management to ensure that accounting records are kept and financial statements are prepared, although they may request the firm to provide assistance. If firm, or network firm, personnel providing such assistance make management decisions, the self-review threat created could not be reduced to an acceptable level by any safeguards. Consequently, personnel should not make such decisions. Examples of such managerial decisions include:

(a) Determining or changing journal entries, or the classifications for accounts or transaction or other accounting records without obtaining the approval of the financial statement audit client;

(b) Authorizing or approving transactions; and

(c) Preparing source documents or originating data (including decisions on valuation assumptions), or making changes to such documents or data.

17.15.3 The audit process involves extensive dialogue between the firm and management of the financial statement audit client. During this process, management requests and receives significant input regarding such matters as accounting principles and financial statement disclosure, the appropriateness of controls and the methods used in determining the stated amounts of assets and liabilities. Technical assistance of this nature and advice on accounting principles for financial statement audit clients are an appropriate means to promote the fair presentation of the financial statements. The provision of such advice does not generally threaten the firm's independence. Similarly, the financial statement audit process may involve assisting an audit client in resolving account reconciliation problems, analyzing and accumulating information for regulatory reporting, assisting in the preparation of consolidated financial statements (including the translation of local statutory accounts to comply with group accounting policies and the transition to a different reporting framework such as International Financial Reporting Standards), drafting disclosure items, proposing adjusting journal entries and providing assistance and advice in the preparation of local statutory accounts of subsidiary entities. These services are considered to be a normal part of the audit process and do not, under normal circumstances, threaten independence.

17.16.0 General Provisions

17.16.1 The examples in these paragraphs indicate that self-review threats may be created if the firm is involved in the preparation of accounting records or financial statements and those financial statements are subsequently the subject matter information of an audit engagement of the firm. This notion may be equally applicable in situations when the subject matter information of the assurance engagement is not financial statements. For example, a self-review threat would be created if the firm developed and prepared prospective financial information and subsequently provided assurance on this prospective financial information. Consequently, the firm should evaluate the significance of any self-review threat created by the provision of such services. If the self-review threat is other than clearly insignificant safeguards should be considered and applied as necessary to reduce the threat to an acceptable level.

17.17.0 Financial Statements Audit Clients That Are Not Quoted Entities

17.17.1 The firm, or a network firm, may provide a financial statement audit client that is not a listed entity with accounting and bookkeeping services, including payroll services, of a routine or mechanical nature, provided any self-review threat created is reduced to an acceptable level. Examples of such services include:

(a)   Recording transactions for which the audit client has determined or approved the appropriate account classification;

(b) Posting coded transactions to the audit client's general ledger;

(c)   Preparing financial statements based on information in the trial balance; and   (d) Posting the audit client approved entries to the trial balance. The significance of any threat created should be evaluated and, if the threat is other than clearly insignificant, safeguards should be considered and applied as necessary to reduce the threat to an acceptable level. Such safeguards might include:

(e) Making arrangements so a member of the assurance team does not perform such services;

(f) Implementing policies and procedures to prohibit the individual providing such services from making any managerial decisions on behalf of the audit client;

(g) Requiring the source data for the accounting entries to be originated by the audit client;

(h) Requiring the underlying assumptions to be originated and approved by the audit client; or

(i)   Obtaining audit client approval for any proposed journal entries or other changes affecting the financial statements.

17.18.0 Financial Statement Audit Clients That are Listed Entities

17.18.1   The provision of accounting and book keeping services, including payroll services and the preparation of financial statements or financial information which forms the basis of the financial statements on which the audit report is provided, on behalf of a financial statement audit client that is a listed entity, may impair the independence of the firm or network firm, or at least give the appearance of impairing independence. Accordingly, no safeguard other than the prohibition of such services, except in emergency situations and when the services fall within the statutory audit mandate, could reduce the threat created to an acceptable level. Therefore, a firm or a network firm should not, with the   limited exceptions below, provide such services to a listed entity that is a financial statement audit client.

17.18.2 The provision of accounting and bookkeeping services of a routine or mechanical nature to divisions or subsidiaries of a financial statement audit client that is a listed entity would not be seen as impairing independence with respect to the audit client provided that the following conditions are met:

(a) The services do not involve the exercise of judgment.

(b) The divisions or subsidiaries for which the service is provided are collectively immaterial to the audit client, or the services provided are collectively immaterial to the division or subsidiary.   (c) The fees to the firm, or network firm, from such services are collectively clearly insignificant. If such services are provided, all of the following safeguards should be applied:

(d) The firm, or network firm, should not assume any managerial role nor make any managerial decisions.

(e) The audit client should accept responsibility for the results of the work.   (f) Personnel providing the services should not participate in the audit.

17.19.0 Emergency Situations

17.19.1   The provision of accounting and bookkeeping services to financial statement audit clients in emergency or other unusual situations, when it is impractical for the audit client to make other arrangements, would not be considered to pose an unacceptable threat to independence provided: (a) The firm, or network firm, does not assume any managerial role or make any managerial decisions;   (b) The audit client accepts responsibility for the results of the work; and

(c) Personnel providing the services are not members of the assurance team.

17.20.0   Valuation Services

17.20.1   A valuation comprises the making of assumptions with regard to future developments, the application of certain methodologies and techniques, and the combination of both in order to compute a certain value, or range of values, for an asset, a liability or for a business as a whole.

17.20.2   A self-review threat may be created when a firm or network firm performs a valuation for a financial statement audit client that is to be incorporated into the client's financial statements.

17.20.3   If the valuation service involves the valuation of matters material to the financial   statements and the valuation involves a significant degree of subjectivity, the self-review threat created could not be reduced to an acceptable level by the application of any safeguard. Accordingly, such valuation services should not be provided or, alternatively, the only course of action would be to withdraw from the financial statement audit engagement.

17.20.4 Performing valuation services for a financial statement audit client that are neither   separately, nor in the aggregate, material to the financial statements, or that do not involve a significant degree of subjectivity, may create a self-review threat that could be reduced to an acceptable level by the application of safeguards. Such safeguards might include:

(a) Involving an additional professional accountant who was not a member of the   assurance team to review the work done or otherwise advise as necessary;   (b) Confirming with the audit client their understanding of the underlying   assumptions of the valuation and the methodology to be used and obtaining   approval for their use;

(c)   Obtaining the audit client's acknowledgement of responsibility for the results of the work performed by the firm; and

(d) Making arrangements so that personnel providing such services do not participate in   the audit engagement. In determining whether the above safeguards would be effective, consideration should be given to the following matters:

(i) The extent of the audit client's knowledge, experience and ability to evaluate the issues concerned, and the extent of their involvement in determining and approving significant matters of judgment.

(ii) The degree to which established methodologies and professional guidelines are applied when performing a particular valuation service.   (iii) For valuations involving standard or established methodologies, the degree of subjectivity inherent in the item concerned. (iv) The reliability and extent of the underlying data.

(v) The degree of dependence on future events of a nature that could create significant volatility inherent in the amounts involved. (vi) The extent and clarity of the disclosures in the financial statements.

17.20.5   When a firm, or a network firm, performs a valuation service for a financial statement audit client for the purposes of making a filing or return to a tax authority, computing an amount of tax due by the client, or for the purpose of tax planning, this would not create a significant threat to independence because such valuations are generally subject to external review, for example by a tax authority.

17.20.6   When the firm performs a valuation that forms part of the subject matter information of   an assurance engagement that is not a financial statement audit engagement, the firm should consider any self-review threats. If the threat is other than clearly insignificant, safeguards should be considered and applied as necessary to eliminate the threat or   reduce it to an acceptable level.

17.21.0   Provision of Taxation Services to Financial Statement Audit Clients

17.21.1 In many jurisdictions, the firm may be asked to provide taxation services to a financial statement audit client. Taxation services comprise a broad range of services, including compliance, planning, provision of formal taxation opinions and assistance in the resolution of tax disputes. Such assignments are generally not seen to create threats to independence.

17.22.0   Provision of Internal Audit Services to Financial Statement Audit Clients

17.22.1 A self-review threat may be created when a firm, or network firm, provides internal audit services to a financial statement audit client. Internal audit services may comprise an extension of the firm's audit service beyond requirements of generally accepted auditing standards, assistance in the performance of a client's internal audit activities or outsourcing of the activities. In evaluating any threats to independence, the nature of the service will need to be considered. For this purpose, internal audit services do not include operational internal audit services unrelated to the internal accounting controls, financial systems or financial statements.

17.22.2 Services involving an extension of the procedures required to conduct a financial   statement audit in accordance with International Standards on Auditing would not be considered to impair independence with respect to the audit client provided that the firm's or network firm's personnel do not act or appear to act in a capacity equivalent to a member of audit Client Management

17.22.3 When the firm, or a network firm, provides assistance in the performance of a   financial statement audit client's internal audit activities or undertakes the outsourcing of some of the activities, any self-review threat created may be reduced to an acceptable level by ensuring that there is a clear separation between the management and *control of the internal audit by client management and the internal audit activities themselves.*

17.22.4 Performing a significant portion of the financial statement audit client's internal audit activities may create a self-review threat and a firm, or network firm, should consider the threats and proceed with caution before taking on such activities. Appropriate safeguards should be put in place and the firm, or network firm, should, in particular, ensure that the audit client acknowledges its responsibilities for establishing, maintaining and monitoring the system of internal controls.

17.22.5 Safeguards that should be applied in all circumstances to reduce any threats created to an acceptable level include ensuring that: (a)   The audit client is responsible for internal audit activities and acknowledges its responsibility for establishing, maintaining and monitoring the system of internal controls;   b) The audit client designates a competent employee, preferably within senior management, to be responsible for internal audit activities;   (c)   The audit client, the audit committee or supervisory body approves the scope, risk and frequency of internal audit work;

(d)   The audit client is responsible for evaluating and determining which recommendations of the firm should be implemented;   (e)   The audit client evaluates the adequacy of the internal audit procedures performed and the findings resulting from the performance of those procedures by, among other things, obtaining and acting on reports from the firm; and   (f) The findings and recommendations resulting from the internal audit activities are reported appropriately to the audit committee or supervisory body.

17.22.6   Consideration should also be given to whether such non-assurance services should be provided only by personnel not involved in the financial statement audit engagement and with different reporting lines within the firm.

17. 23.0   Provision of IT Systems Services to Financial Statement Audit Clients

17.23.1   The provision of services by a firm or network firm to a financial statement audit client that involve the design and implementation of financial information technology systems that are used to generate information forming part of a client's financial statements may create a self-review threat.   17.23.2 The self-review threat is likely to be too significant to allow the provision of such services to a financial statement audit client unless appropriate safeguards are put in place ensuring that:

(a)   The audit client acknowledges its responsibility for establishing and monitoring a system of internal controls;

(b)   The audit client designates a competent employee, preferably within senior management, with the responsibility to make all management decisions with respect to the design and implementation of the hardware or software system;

(c)   The audit client makes all management decisions with respect to the design and implementation process;

(d)   The audit client evaluates the adequacy and results of the design and implementation of the system; and

(e) The audit client is responsible for the operation of the system (hardware or software) and the data used or generated by the system.   17.23.3 Consideration should

also be given to whether such non-assurance services should be provided only by personnel not involved in the financial statement audit engagement   and with different reporting lines within the firm.

        17.23.4   The provision of services by a firm, or network firm, to a financial statement audit   client which involve either the design or the implementation of financial information technology systems that are used to generate information forming part of a client's financial statements may also create a self-review threat. The significance of the threat, if any, should be evaluated and, if the threat is other than clearly insignificant, safeguards should be considered and applied as necessary to eliminate the threat or reduce it to an acceptable level.   **17.23.5**   The provision of services in connection with the assessment, design and implementation   of internal accounting controls and risk management controls are not considered to create a threat to independence provided that firm or network firm personnel do not perform management functions.

        17.24.0 Temporary Staff Assignments to Financial Statement Audit Clients

        17.24.1 The lending of staff by a firm, or network firm, to a financial statement audit client may create a self-review threat when the individual is in a position to influence the preparation of a client's accounts or financial statements. In practice, such assistance may be given (particularly in emergency situations) but only on the understanding that the firm's or network firm's personnel will not be involved in: (a) Making management decisions;   (b) Approving or signing agreements or other similar documents; or

        (c) Exercising discretionary authority to commit the client.

        17.24.2   Each situation should be carefully analyzed to identify whether any threats are   created and whether appropriate safeguards should be implemented. Safeguards that should be applied in all circumstances to reduce any threats to an acceptable level include:

        (a) The staff providing the assistance should not be given audit responsibility for any function or activity that they performed or supervised during their temporary staff assignment; and

        (b)   The audit client should acknowledge its responsibility for directing and supervising the activities of firm, or network firm, personnel.

        17.25.0   Provision of Litigation Support Services to Financial Statement Audit Clients.

        17.25.1   Litigation support services may include activities such as acting as an expert witness, calculating estimated damages or other amounts that might become receivable or payable as the result of litigation or other legal dispute, and assistance with document management and retrieval in relation to a dispute or litigation.

        17.25.2   A self-review threat may be created when the litigation support services provided to a financial statement audit client include the estimation of the possible outcome and thereby affects the amounts or disclosures to be reflected in the financial statements. The significance of any threat created will depend upon factors such as: (a) The materiality of the amounts involved;   (b) The degree of subjectivity inherent in the matter concerned; and   (c) The nature of the engagement.

17.25.3   The firm, or network firm, should evaluate the significance of any threat created and, if the threat is other than clearly insignificant, safeguards should be considered and applied as necessary to eliminate the threat or reduce it to an acceptable level. Such safeguards might include:

(a) Policies and procedures to prohibit individuals assisting the audit client from making managerial decisions on behalf of the client;   (b) Using professionals who are not members of the assurance team to perform the service; or (c) The involvement of others, such as independent experts.

17.25.4 If the role undertaken by the firm or network firm involved making managerial decisions on behalf of the financial statement audit client, the threats created could not be reduced to an acceptable level by the application of any safeguard. Therefore, the firm or network firm should not perform this type of service for an audit client.

17.26.0 Recruiting Senior Management

17.26.1 The recruitment of senior management for an assurance client, such as those in a position to affect the subject matter information of the assurance engagement, may create current or future self-interest, familiarity and intimidation threats. The significance of the threat will depend upon factors such as: (a) The role of the person to be recruited; and (b) The nature of the assistance sought.

17.26.2 The firm could generally provide such services as reviewing the professional qualifications of a number of applicants and provide advice on their suitability for the post. In addition, the firm could generally produce a short-list of candidates for interview, provided it has been drawn up using criteria specified by the assurance client.

17.26.3 The significance of the threat created should be evaluated and, if the threat is other than clearly insignificant, safeguards should be considered and applied as necessary to reduce the threat to an acceptable level. In all cases, the firm should not make management decisions and the decision as to whom to hire should be left to the client.

17.27.0 Corporate Finance and Similar Activities

17.27.1 The provision of corporate finance services, advice or assistance to an assurance client may create advocacy and self-review threats. In the case of certain corporate finance services, the independence threats created would be so significant no safeguards could be applied to reduce the threats to an acceptable level. For example, promoting, dealing in, or underwriting of an assurance client's shares is not compatible with providing assurance services. Moreover, committing the assurance client to the terms of a transaction or consummating a transaction on behalf of the client would create a threat to independence so significant no safeguard could reduce the threat to an acceptable level. In the case of a financial statement audit client the provision of those corporate finance services referred to above by a firm or a network firm would create a threat to independence so significant no safeguard could reduce the threat to an acceptable level.

17.27.2 Other corporate finance services may create advocacy or self-review threats; however, safeguards may be available to reduce these threats to an acceptable level. Examples of such services include assisting a client in developing corporate strategies, assisting in identifying or introducing a client to possible sources of capital that meet the client specifications or criteria, and providing structuring advice and assisting a client in analyzing the accounting effects of proposed transactions. Safeguards that should be considered include:

(a) Policies and procedures to prohibit individuals assisting the assurance client from   making managerial decisions on behalf of the client;

(b) Using professionals who are not members of the assurance team to provide the   services; and (c) Ensuring the firm does not commit the assurance client to the terms of any   transaction or consummate a transaction on behalf of the client.

17.28.0 Fees and Pricing   Fees–Relative Size

17.28.1 When the total fees generated by an assurance client represent a large proportion of a firm's total fees, the dependence on that client or client group and concern about the possibility of losing the client may create a self-interest threat. The significance of the threat will depend upon factors such as: (a) The structure of the firm; and   (b) Whether the firm is well established or newly created.

17.28.2   The significance of the threat should be evaluated and, if the threat is other than clearly insignificant, safeguards should be considered and applied as necessary to reduce the threat to an acceptable level. Such safeguards might include:

(a) Discussing the extent and nature of fees charged with the audit committee, or others charged with governance;   (b) Taking steps to reduce dependency on the client; (c) External quality control reviews; and   (d) Consulting a third party, such as a professional regulatory body or another professional accountant.

17.28.3   A Self-interest threat may also be created when the fees generated by the assurance   client represent a large proportion of the revenue of an individual partner. The significance of the threat should be evaluated and, if the threat is other than clearly insignificant, safeguards should be considered and applied as necessary to reduce the threat to an acceptable level. Such safeguards might include: (a) Policies and procedures to monitor and implement quality control of assurance   engagements; and

(b) Involving an additional professional accountant who was not a member of the assurance team to review the work done or otherwise advise as necessary.

17.29.0 Fees–Overdue

17.29.1 A self-interest threat may be created if fees due from an assurance client for professional services remain unpaid for a long time, especially if a significant part is not paid before the issue of the assurance report for the following year. Generally the payment of such fees should be required before the report is issued. The following safeguards may be applicable:

(a) Discussing the level of outstanding fees with the audit committee, or others charged with governance. (b) Involving an additional professional accountant who did not take part in the assurance engagement to provide advice or review the work performed.

17.29.2   The firm should also consider whether the overdue fees might be regarded as being   equivalent to a loan to the client and whether, because of the significance of the overdue fees, it is appropriate for the firm to be re-appointed.

17.30.0 Pricing

17.30.1   *When a firm obtains an assurance engagement at a significantly lower fee level than that charged by the predecessor firm, or quoted by other firms, the self-interest threat created will not be reduced to an acceptable level unless: (a) The firm is able to demonstrate that appropriate time and qualified staff are assigned to the task; and (b) All applicable assurance standards, guidelines and quality control procedures are being complied with.*

17.31.0   *Contingent Fees*

17.31.1 *Contingent fees are fees calculated on a predetermined basis relating to the   outcome   or   result of a transaction or the result of the work performed. For the purposes of this section, fees are not regarded as being contingent if a court or other public authority has established them.*

17.31.2 *A contingent fee charged by a firm in respect of an assurance engagement creates self- interest and advocacy threats that cannot be reduced to an acceptable level by the application of any safeguard. Accordingly, a firm should not enter into any fee arrangement for an assurance engagement under which the amount of the fee is contingent on the result of the assurance work or on items that are the subject matter information of the assurance engagement.*

17.31.3 *A contingent fee charged by a firm in respect of a non-assurance service provided to an assurance client may also create self-interest and advocacy threats. If the amount of the fee for a non-assurance engagement was agreed to, or contemplated, during an assurance engagement and was contingent on the result of that assurance engagement, the threats could not be reduced to an acceptable level by the application of any safeguard. Accordingly, the only acceptable action is not to accept such arrangements. For other types of contingent fee arrangements, the significance of the threats created will depend on factors such as:*

(a) The range of possible fee amounts; (b) The degree of variability; (c) The basis on which the fee is to be determined; (d) Whether the outcome or result of the transaction is to be reviewed by an Independent third party; and (d) The effect of the event or transaction on the assurance engagement.

17.31.4   *The significance of the threats should be evaluated and, if the threats are other than clearly insignificant, safeguards should be considered and applied as necessary to reduce the threats to an acceptable level. Such safeguards might include:*

(a) Disclosing to the audit committee, or others charged with governance, the extent and nature of fees charged;   (b) Review or determination of the final fee by an unrelated third party; or (c) Quality and control policies and procedures.

17. 32.0 *Gifts and Hospitality*

17.32.1 *Accepting gifts or hospitality from an assurance client may create self-interest and familiarity threats. When a firm or a member of the assurance team accepts gifts or hospitality, unless the value is clearly insignificant, the threats to independence cannot be reduced to an acceptable level by the application of any safeguard. Consequently, a firm or a member of the assurance team should not accept such gifts or hospitality.   17 33.0 Actual or Threatened Litigation*

17.33.1   When litigation takes place, or appears likely, between the firm or a member of the assurance team and the assurance client, a self-interest or intimidation threat may be created. The relationship between client management and the members of the assurance team must be characterized by complete candor and full disclosure regarding all aspects of a client's business operations. The firm and the client's management may be placed in adversarial positions by litigation, affecting management's willingness to make complete disclosures and the firm may face a self-interest threat. The significance of the threat created will depend upon such factors as: (a) The materiality of the litigation;   (b) The nature of the assurance engagement; and   (c) Whether the litigation relates to a prior assurance engagement.

17.33.2   Once the significance of the threat has been evaluated the following safeguards should be applied, if necessary, to reduce the threats to an acceptable level:

(a) Disclosing to the audit committee, or others charged with governance, the extent and nature of the litigation;

(b) If the litigation involves a member of the assurance team, removing that individual from the assurance team; or

(c) Involving an additional professional accountant in the firm who was not a member of the assurance team to review the work done or otherwise advise as necessary. If such safeguards do not reduce the threat to an appropriate level, the only appropriate action is to withdraw from, or refuse to accept, the assurance engagement.

CHAPTER EIGHTEEN

18.1.0 OBJECTIVITY AND INDEPENDENCE IN FINANCIAL REPORTING AND SIMILAR NON-AUDIT ROLES. 18.1.1 There are roles other than the audit in which a member is required to report with similar authority on financial matters, and to which therefore the consideration referred to in Chapter 17 (above) apply, as follows; (a) Financial reporting The considerations, which make it essential for a member's objectivity to be safeguarded when he carries out an audit are also relevant to other financial reporting assignments requiring a professional opinion, including reporting assignments where a document has been prepared in contemplation that a third   party may rely on it. Some reports are commissioned by management for management's internal use only, these are not subject to the same rules.

(b) Litigation support   A member called upon to report or undertake work in connection with civil proceeding or with criminal prosecution should appreciate that such work may be tendered as evidence in a court of law and/or involve the member in giving evidence upon oath. The objectivity of such a member should, therefore, be safeguarded when he accepts and carries on such an assignment.

(c) Specialist valuation The objectivity of a member, who carries out a specialist valuation, the results of which may be included in financial accounts or public documents, needs to be safeguarded, and similar considerations apply to those set out in Part 3 and shall be read in conjunction with 3(1) together in relation to the carrying out of an audit.

18.2.0 OBJECTIVITY AND INDEPENDENCE IN PROFESSIONAL ROLES OTHER THAN THOSE COVERED IN Paragraph 17.1.0
18.2.1 This Section deals with work other than the work covered by paragraph 3 and 16 of this code including but not limited to (a) Taxation services; (b) Preparation of accounts; (c) Corporate advisory services other than the preparation of documents for public use; (d) Management consultancy services; (e) Reporting to management/ secondment to management.; and (f) Receivership and Insolvency Services.
113
18.2.2 Independence in the sense in which it is sometimes applied to audit assignments is not essential to the work referred to in the previous paragraph, provided that the practice is not also auditor to the client and objectivity is not impaired.
18.2.3 There are nevertheless certain factors which by their nature are a threat to objectivity in any professional role. Accordingly, the following considerations referred to in chapter16 (above) apply to the professional assignments referred to in paragraph 18.2.1 above.
18.2.4 Area of risk - family and other personal relationships An objective approach to any assignment may be subject to self-interest or familiarity threats as a consequence of a family or other close personal or business relationship.
Objectivity in relation to any assignment may be subject to a self-interest threat where a mutual business interest exists with a client company or with an officer or employee of the company. The safeguards indicated in paragraph 16.3.1 (a(b)(c) of chapter 16 should be implemented as appropriate. In addition, adequate disclosure of any conflict of interest arising should be made to all relevant parties.
18.3.0 Area of risk - loans (a) An objective approach to any assignment may be subject to a self- interest threat if a firm or any principal in the firm should directly or indirectly make any loan to or receive a loan from a client, or give or accept any guarantee in relation to a debt of the client, firm or principal. (b) Firm or a principal of the firm should not receive any loan from a client. This is because the size of the perceived self-interest threat arising in such circumstances is generally seen as being too great to be offset by any available safeguards. Nor should a firm or principal make any loan to a client, although this restriction does not normally apply to any account in credit with a client clearing bank or similar financial institution.
(c) The above advice is not intended to preclude a loan, overdraft or home mortgage being accepted from a client financial institution in the normal course of business and on normal commercial terms provided that where the loan is applied so as to subscribe to partnership capital or where the loan is made to an engagement partner, the significance of the loan is not such as to cast doubt on the objectivity of the practice in performing the role or roles which it is contracted to discharge.
(d) Similar considerations apply where there are significant overdue fees from a client or group of connected clients.
18.3.1 Area of risk - goods and services: hospitality or other benefits A self- interest threat arises where anyone in the firm receives goods, services or hospitality from a

client. This should not, therefore, be accepted by a firm or by anyone closely connected with it, unless the value of any benefit is insignificant.

18.3.2 Beneficial interests in shares and other investments A self-interest threat to the objectivity of a member or firm will arise in relation to any investment in a company or undertaking with which the firm has a professional relationship, and the safeguards set out in paragraphs 16.1.12 to 16.1.15 above should be implemented as appropriate. Where the value of the investment is material to the financial circumstances of the investing member or firm, they should cease to advise professionally (see paragraph 16.1.13.)

18.3.3 Business advisers Where a member or a practice acts as business adviser to a client, he, or it may invest in that client, and if the client is a company, act as sponsor or promoter of its shares, provided that the relation-ship is clearly disclosed to relevant parties.

18.3.4 Discussion Members who hold office in a client company, or have comparable business relationship with a client, should be aware of the dangers inherent in seeking to combine such a role with that of adviser, having regard to the self-interest threat to their objectivity.

In such circumstances, members should be aware of the distinctive nature of each of the roles in which they are professionally engaged and employ safeguards including disclosure where appropriate.

18.3.5 Arbitration It is a requirement of law that an arbitrator must act independently of the parties on the issues involved in arbitration. Members should ensure independence in fact and in appearance in any such situation.

18.3.6 Insolvency And Receivership Services: It should be noted that the statutory obligations as provided by CAMA in respect of Winding Up proceedings Sections 401- 540 of CAMA apply to members offering Insolvency and receivership services. It is also pertinent to note that Reconstruction, i.e. Amalgamation, Mergers and Takeover of Companies and Corporations are services also undertaken by members of the institute. The Rules governing this practice is covered by the procedures in Sections 590-613 of CAMA. Members should also be aware of the SEC Rules and Guidelines.

CHAPTER NINETEEN
19.1.0 CONSULTANCY
This Statement applies only to practising members, affiliates and, where appropriate, employees of practising firms.

19.1.1 If a member in practice (the practitioner) obtains the advice of a member (the consultant) on a consultancy basis on behalf of a client, the consultant or any practising firm with which he or his consultancy organisation is associated should not, without the consent of the practitioner, accept from that client within two years of completion of the consultancy assignment any work which was, at the time the consultant was first retained in relation to that client's affairs, being carried out by the practitioner.

19.1.2 The same considerations apply where a practitioner introduces one of his clients to the consultant for the purpose of consultancy.

19.1.3 The Chartered Accountant in public practice may in addition to assurance services work in the areas listed in Chapter 18.2.1 above provided he complies with the relevant provision of the Code.

PART THREE

CHAPTER TWENTY
20.1.0 MEMBERS IN BUSINESS
   Introduction
   20.1.1 This Part of the Code illustrates how the conceptual framework contained in Part one is to be applied by Chartered Accountants in business.

   20.1.2   Investors, creditors, employers and other sectors of the business community, as well as governments and the public at large, may rely on the work of Chartered Accountants in business. Chartered Accountants in business may be solely or jointly responsible for the preparation and reporting of financial and other information, which both their employing organizations and third parties may rely on. They may also be responsible for providing effective financial management and competent advice on a variety of business-related matters.

   20.1.3   Chartered Accountants in business may be salaried employees, partners, directors (whether executive or non-executive), owner managers, volunteers or others working for one or more employing organizations. The legal form of the relationship with the employing organization, if any, has no bearing on the ethical responsibilities incumbent on the Chartered Accountant in business.

   20.1.4   Chartered Accountants in business have a responsibility to further the legitimate aims of their employing organizations. This Code does not seek to hinder Chartered Accountants in business from properly fulfilling that responsibility, but considers circumstances in which conflicts may be created with the absolute duty to comply with the fundamental principles.

   20.1.5   Chartered Accountants in business often hold senior positions within organizations. The more senior the position, the greater will be the ability and opportunity to influence events, practices and attitudes. Chartered Accountants in business are expected, therefore, to encourage an ethics-based culture in an employing organization that emphasises the importance that senior management places on ethical behaviour.

   20.1.6   The examples presented in the following sections are intended to illustrate how the conceptual framework is to be applied and are not intended to be, nor should they be interpreted as, an exhaustive list of all circumstances experienced by Chartered Accountants in business that may create threats to compliance with the principles. Consequently, it is not sufficient for Chartered Accountants in business merely to

117

comply with the examples; rather, the framework should be applied to the particular circumstances faced.

20.1.7   Threats and Safeguards   Compliance with the fundamental principles may potentially be threatened by a broad   range of circumstances. Many threats fall into the following categories: (a) Self-interest; (b) Self-review; (c) Advocacy; (d)Familiarity; and (e) Intimidation.   These threats were discussed further in Part 2 of this Code.

20.1.8 Examples of circumstances that may create self-interest threats for Chartered Accountants in business include, but are not limited to: (a) Financial interests, loans or guarantees.   (b)Incentive compensation arrangements.   (c)Inappropriate personal use of corporate assets. (d) Concern over employment security. (e) Commercial pressure from outside the employing organization.

20.1.9 Circumstances that may create self-review threats include, but are not limited to, business decisions or data being subject to review and justification by the same Chartered Accountant in business responsible for making those decisions or preparing that data.

20.1.10 When furthering the legitimate goals and objectives of their employing organizations Chartered Accountants in business may promote the organization's position, provided any statements made are neither false nor misleading. Such actions generally would not create an advocacy threat.

20.1.11 Examples of circumstances that may create familiarity threats include, but are not limited to: (a) Chartered Accountants in business in a position to influence financial or nonfinancial reporting or business decisions having an immediate or close family member who is in a position to benefit from that influence. (b) Long association with business contacts influencing business decisions. (c) Acceptance of a gift or preferential treatment, unless the value is clearly insignificant.

20.1.12 Examples of circumstances that may create intimidation threats include, but are not limited to:

118

(a) Threat of dismissal or replacement of Chartered Accountants in business or a close or immediate family member over a disagreement about the application of an accounting principle or the way in which financial information is to be reported.

(b) A dominant personality attempting to influence the decision making process, for example with regard to the awarding of contracts or the application of an accounting principle.

20.1.13   Chartered Accountants in business may also find that specific circumstances give rise to unique threats to compliance with one or more of the fundamental principles. Such unique threats obviously cannot be categorized. In all professional and business relationships, Chartered Accountants in business should always be on the alert for such circumstances and threats.

20.1.14 Safeguards that may eliminate or reduce to an acceptable level the threats faced by Chartered Accountants in business fall into two broad categories: (a)

Safeguards created by the profession, legislation or regulation; and (b) Safeguards in the work environment.

    20.1.15 Examples of safeguards created by the profession, legislation or regulation are detailed in paragraph 3.2.8 of chapter three of this Code.

    20.1.16 Safeguards in the work environment include, but are not restricted to: (a) The employing organization's systems of corporate oversight or other oversight Structures. E.g. Compliance functions (b) The employing organization's ethics and conduct programmes. (c) Recruitment procedures in the employing organization emphasizing the importance of employing high caliber competent staff. (d) Strong internal controls. (e) Appropriate disciplinary processes. (f) Leadership that stresses the importance of ethical behavior and the expectation those employees will act in an ethical manner. (g) Policies and procedures to implement and monitor the quality of employee performance. (h) Timely communication of the employing organization's policies and procedures, including any changes to them, to all employees and appropriate training and education on such policies and procedures. (i) Policies and procedures to empower and encourage employees to communicate to senior levels within the employing organization any ethical issues that concern them without fear of retribution. (j) Consultation with other appropriate professional accountants.

    20.1.17 In circumstances where a Chartered Accountants in business believe that unethical behavior or actions by others will continue to occur within the employing organization, the

    Chartered Accountant in business should consider seeking legal advice. In those extreme situations where all available safeguards have been exhausted and it is not possible to reduce the threat to an acceptable level, Chartered Accountants in business shall conclude that it is appropriate to resign from the employing organization.

    20.2.0 Potential Conflicts

    20.2.1 Chartered Accountants in business have a professional obligation to comply with the fundamental principles. There may be times, however, when their responsibilities to an employing organisation and the professional obligations to comply with the fundamental principles are in conflict. Ordinarily, Chartered Accountants in business should support the legitimate and ethical objectives established by the employer and the rules and procedures drawn up in support of those objectives. Nevertheless, where compliance with the fundamental principles is threatened, Chartered Accountants in business must consider a response to the circumstances.

    20.2.2 As a consequence of responsibilities to an employing organization, Chartered Accountants in business may be under pressure to act or behave in ways that could directly or indirectly threaten compliance with the fundamental principles. Such pressure may be explicit or implicit; it may come from a supervisor, manager, director or another individual within the employing organization. Chartered Accountants in Business may face pressure to: (a) Act contrary to laws or regulations. (b) Act contrary to technical or professional standards. (c) Facilitate unethical or illegal earnings management strategies. (d) Lie to, or otherwise intentionally mislead (including misleading by remaining silent) others, in particular: (i) The auditors of the employing organization; or (ii) Regulators.

(e) Issue, or otherwise be associated with, a financial or non-financial report that materially misrepresents the facts, including statements in connection with, for example:

(i) The financial statements; (ii) Tax compliance; (iii) Legal compliance; or (iv) Reports required by securities regulators.

20.2.3 The significance of threats arising from such pressures, such as intimidation threats, should be evaluated and, if they are other than clearly insignificant, safeguards should be considered and applied as necessary to eliminate them or reduce them to an acceptable level. Such safeguards may include:

120

(a) Obtaining advice where appropriate from within the employing organisation, an independent professional adviser or a relevant professional body. (d) The existence of a formal dispute resolution process within the employing organization. (e) Seeking legal advice. Preparation and Reporting of Information

20.2.4 Chartered Accountants in business are often involved in the preparation and reporting of information that may either be made public or used by others inside or outside the employing organization. Such information may include financial or management information, for example, forecasts and budgets, financial statements, management discussion and analysis, and the management letter of representation provided to the auditors as part of an audit of financial statements. Chartered Accountant in business should prepare or present such information fairly, honestly and in accordance with relevant professional standards so that the information will be understood in its context.

20.2.5 Chartered Accountants in business who have the responsibility for the preparation or approval of the general purpose financial statements of an employing organization should ensure that those financial statements are presented in accordance with the applicable financial reporting standards.

20.2.6 Chartered Accountants in business should maintain information for which they responsible in a manner that: (a) Describes clearly the true nature of business transactions, assets or liabilities; (b) Classifies and records information in a timely and proper manner; and (c) Represents the facts accurately and completely in all material respects.

20.2.7 Threats to compliance with the fundamental principles, for example self-interest or intimidation threats to objectivity or professional competence and due care, may be created where Chartered Accountants in business may be pressured (either externally or by the possibility of personal gain) to become associated with misleading information or to become associated with misleading information through the actions of others.

20.2.8 The significance of such threats will depend on factors such as the source of the pressure and the degree to which the information is, or may be, misleading. The significance of the threats should be evaluated and, if they are other than clearly insignificant, safeguards should be considered and applied as necessary to eliminate them *or reduce them to an acceptable level. Such safeguards may include consultation with superiors within the employing organization, for example, the audit committee or other body responsible for governance, or with a relevant professional body.*

20.2.9 Where it is not possible to reduce the threat to an acceptable level, Chartered Accountants in business should refuse to remain associated with information they consider is or may be misleading. Should the Chartered Accountant in business be aware
     121
that the issuance of misleading information is either significant or persistent, the Chartered Accountant in business should consider informing appropriate authorities in line with the guidance in paragraph 1.2.4. The Chartered Accountant in business may also wish to seek legal advice or resign.

20.3.0 Acting with Sufficient Expertise

20.3.1 The fundamental principle of professional competence and due care requires that Chartered Accountants in business should only undertake significant tasks for which the Chartered Accountant in business has, or can obtain, sufficient specific training or experience. Chartered Accountants in business should not intentionally mislead an employer as to the level of expertise or experience possessed, nor should Chartered Accountant in business fail to seek appropriate expert advice and assistance when required.

20.3.2 Circumstances that threaten the ability of Chartered Accountant in business to perform duties with the appropriate degree of professional competence and due care includes: • Insufficient time for properly performing or completing the relevant duties. • Incomplete, restricted or otherwise inadequate information for performing the duties properly. • Insufficient experience, training and/or education. • Inadequate resources for the proper performance of the duties.

20.3.3 The significance of such threats will depend on factors such as the extent to which the Chartered Accountant in business is working with others, relative seniority in the business and the level of supervision and review applied to the work. The significance of the threats should be evaluated and, if they are other than clearly insignificant, safeguards should be considered and applied as necessary to eliminate them or reduce them to an acceptable level. Safeguards that may be considered include: • Obtaining additional advice or training. • Ensuring that there is adequate time available for performing the relevant duties. • Obtaining assistance from someone with the necessary expertise. • Consulting, where appropriate, with: -Superiors within the employing organization;   -Independent experts; or   -A relevant professional body.

20.3.4 Where threats cannot be eliminated or reduced to an acceptable level, Chartered Accountants in business should consider whether to refuse to perform the duties in question. If a Chartered Accountant business determines that refusal is appropriate the reasons for doing so should be clearly communicated
     122
20.4.0 Financial Interests

20.4.1 Chartered Accountants in business may have financial interests, or may know of financial interests of immediate or close family members, that could, in certain circumstances, give rise to threats to compliance with the fundamental principles. For example, self- interest threats to objectivity or confidentiality may be created through the existence of the motive and opportunity to manipulate price sensitive information in order to gain financially. Examples of circumstances that may create self-interest threats include, but are not limited to situations where the Chartered Accountant in business or an immediate or close family member:

• *Holds a direct or indirect financial interest in the employing organization and the value of that financial interest could be directly affected by decisions made by the Chartered Accountant in business;*

• *Is eligible for a profit related bonus and the value of that bonus could be directly affected by decisions made by the Chartered Accountant in business;*

• *May qualify for performance related bonuses if certain targets are achieved.*

20.4.2 In evaluating the significance of such a threat, and the appropriate safeguards to be applied to eliminate the threat or reduce it to an acceptable level, Chartered Accountants in business must examine the nature of the financial interest. This includes an evaluation of the significance of the financial interest and whether it is direct or indirect. Clearly, what constitutes a significant or valuable stake in an organization will vary from individual to individual, depending on personal circumstances.

20.4.2 If threats are other than clearly insignificant, safeguards should be considered and applied as necessary to eliminate or reduce them to an acceptable level. Such safeguards may include:

• *Policies and procedures for a committee independent of management to determine the level of form of remuneration of senior management.*

• *Disclosure of all relevant interests, and of any plans to trade in relevant shares to those charged with the governance of the employing organization, in accordance with any internal policies.*

• *Consultation, where appropriate, with superiors within the employing organization.*

• *Consultation, where appropriate, with those charged with the governance of the employing organization or relevant professional bodies.*

123

• *Internal and external procedures.*

• *Up-to-date education on ethical issues and the legal restrictions and other regulations around potential insider trading.*

20.4.4 Chartered Accountants in business should neither manipulate information nor use confidential information for personal gain.

20.5.0 Inducements

Receiving Offers

20.5.1 Chartered Accountants in business or an immediate or close family member may be offered an inducement. Inducements may take various forms, including gifts, hospitality, preferential treatment and inappropriate appeals to friendship or loyalty.

20.5.2   *Offers of inducements may create threats to compliance with the fundamental principles. When a Chartered Accountant in business or an immediate or close family member is offered an inducement, the situation should be carefully considered. Self-interest threats to objectivity or confidentiality are created where an inducement is made in an attempt to unduly influence actions or decisions, encourage illegal or dishonest behavior or obtain confidential information. Intimidation threats to objectivity or confidentiality are created if such an inducement is accepted and it is followed by threats to make that offer public and damage the reputation of either the Chartered Accountant in business or an immediate or close family member.*

20.5.3 *The significance of such threats will depend on the nature, value and intent behind the offer. If a reasonable and informed third party, having knowledge of all relevant information, would consider the inducement insignificant and not intended to encourage unethical behavior, then a Chartered Accountant in business may conclude that the offer is made in the normal course business and may generally conclude that there is no significant threat to compliance with the fundamental principles.*

20.5.4 *If evaluated threats are other than clearly insignificant, safeguards should be considered and applied as necessary to eliminate them or reduce them to an acceptable level. When the threats cannot be eliminated or reduced to an acceptable level through the application of safeguards, a Chartered Accountant in business should not accept the inducement. As the real or apparent threats to compliance with the fundamental principles do not merely arise from acceptance of an inducement but, sometimes, merely from the fact of the offer having been made, additional safeguards should be adopted. Chartered Accountants in business should assess the risk associated with all such offers and consider whether the following actions should be taken:*

(a) Where such offers have been made, immediately inform higher levels of management or those charged with governance of the employing organization;

(b) Inform third parties of the offer – for example, a professional body or the employer of the individual who made the offer; a Chartered Accountant in business should, however, consider seeking legal advice before taking such a step; and

(c)   Advise immediate or close family members of relevant threats and safeguards where they are potentially in positions that might result in offers of inducements, for example as a result of their employment situation; and

(d) Inform higher levels of management or those charged with governance of the employing organization where immediate or close family members are employed by competitors or potential suppliers of that organisation.

20.6.0 *Making Offers*

20.6.1 *Chartered Accountants in business may be in a situation where they are expected to, or are under other pressure to, offer inducements to subordinate the judgment of other individuals or organisations, influence decision-making processes or obtain confidential information.*

20.6.2 *Such pressure may come from within the employing organization, for example, from a colleague or superior. It may also come from an external individual or organization   suggesting actions or business decisions that would be advantageous to the employing organisation possibly influencing the Chartered Accountant in business improperly.*

     20.6.3 Chartered Accountants in business should not offer inducement to improperly influence professional judgment of a third party. 20.6.4 Where the pressure to offer an unethical inducement comes from within the employing organization, the Chartered Accountant should follow the principles and guidance regarding ethical conflict resolution set out in Part One Section 2.3.0 of this Code.

PART FOUR

CHAPTER TWENTY-ONE
21.1.0 ENFORCEMENT OF ETHICAL STANDARDS

     This statement shall apply to all members.

     21.1.1 The power of the Institute to enforce ethical standards is derived from The Institute of Chartered Accountants of Nigeria Act no 15 1965 which power is conferred on the Accountants' Disciplinary Tribunal and the Tribunal in this respect is independent of Council.

     21.1.2 The Investigating Panel considers complaints against the conduct of members, and is empowered to initiate disciplinary action by referring appropriate cases to the Disciplinary Tribunal for adjudication.

     21.1.3 where a complaint is against the conduct of a firm having more than one partner, the complaint shall be deemed to have been made against each and every member who was partner in the said firm at the material time, for the purposes of this statement.

     21.1.4 Any failure to follow the guidance in fundamental principles or in the statements shall also be taken into account by the committee of the Institute responsible for regulating the work of members and member firms.

     21.2.0   ENFORCEMENT PROCEDURES

     21.2.1   Where a complaint is received by the Institute alleging a case of misconduct against a member, such a member shall be requested by the Investigating Panel to furnish his defence or reaction to the complaint within 14 days of the receipt of the request to do so.

     21.2.2 If the member fails to respond within the specified time, a first reminder shall be sent to him requesting him to send his defence or reaction within 7 days from the receipt of the reminder and a warning that non-response shall amount to disrespect to the Institute and is sanctionable by the Disciplinary Tribunal.

     21.2.3   If the member fails to respond after the first reminder, a formal charge shall be preferred against the member before the Disciplinary Tribunal.

     The provisions and/or procedures contained in paragraphs 21.2.1 and 21.2.2 above shall apply to all other requirement or directive of the Panel to a member so that failure or neglect by the member to abide by the requirement or directive shall also be treated as disrespect of the Institute and is sanction able by the Disciplinary Tribunal.

21.2.4   If the member's contact address cannot be readily obtained, The Panel shall publish the invitation in a National Newspaper and if after 14 days there is no response from the member, this shall be treated as disrespect to the Institute and is sanction able by the Disciplinary Tribunal

21.2.5 If having considered the facts before it, and any representation made by the member, the Panel is of the opinion that in all the circumstances those facts amount to misconduct and is of the further opinion that disciplinary proceedings should be brought, it will prefer a formal complaint to the Disciplinary Tribunal.

21.2.6 It is the Disciplinary Tribunal alone that can determine, subject to the right of appeal referred to below, whether a complaint of misconduct is proved.

21.2.7   From the Accountants 'Disciplinary Tribunal, a member has a right of appeal to the Court of Appeal. See Section 12(5) of the Institute of Chartered Accountants of Nigeria Act No 15 of 1965...

21.2.8 Failure of a member to respond to any publication requiring such a member to appear before the Investigating Panel will constitute an act of professional misconduct.

21.2.9 A Member of the Institute who changes his address from the original address he has with the Institute without giving the Institute notice of the change thereof, is deemed to have committed an Act of professional misconduct.

21.2.10 Any member of the Institute who has been declared guilty of Professional Misconduct by the Accountants' Disciplinary Tribunal shall not be eligible either to serve on the Institute's Council or any of the Institute's committees for a period of five (5) years from the date of re-admission into membership.

Discuss 21.2.10 with committee members (if the 5 years is after serving the sentence imposed by the Tribunal or)

DEFINITIONS

In this Code of Ethics for Chartered Accountants, the following expressions have the following meanings assigned to them:

Accountancy Practice - includes Assurance, Investigation, Forensic Accounting, Tax Practice, Consultancy Practice, Insolvency/Receivership and Financial Advisory Services.

Advertising- The communication to the public of information as to the services or skills provided by Chartered Accountants in public practice with a view to procuring professional business.   Assurance Client – means an audit client. Assurance Client: The responsible party that is the person (or persons) who: (a) In a direct reporting engagement, is responsible for the subject matter; or   (b)   In an assertion-based engagement, is responsible for the subject matter information and may be responsible for the subject matter. (For an assurance client that is a financial statement audit client see the definition of financial statement audit client.)

Assurance engagement: An engagement in which a Chartered Accountant in public practice expresses a conclusion designed to enhance the degree of confidence of the intended users other than the responsible party about the outcome of the evaluation or measurement of a subject matter against criteria.

Assurance team (a) All members of the engagement team for the assurance engagement; (b) All others within a firm who can directly influence the outcome of the assurance engagement, including: (i) Those who recommend the compensation of, or who provide direct supervisory, management or other oversight of the assurance engagement partner in connection with the performance of the assurance engagement. For the purposes of a financial statement audit engagement this includes those at all successively senior levels above the engagement partner through the firm's Chief executive;

(ii) Those who provide consultation regarding technical or industry specific issues, transactions or events for the assurance engagement; and

(iii) Those who provide quality control for the assurance engagement, including those who perform the engagement quality control review for the assurance engagement; and.

(b) For the purposes of a financial statement audit client, all those within a network firm who can directly influence the outcome of the financial statement audit engagement.

Bare Trustees:

Comments- These are explanatory statements on areas or issues where doubts exist.

Chartered Accountant: An individual who is a member of The Institute of Chartered Accountants of Nigeria.

Chartered Accountant in business: A Chartered Accountant employed or engaged in an executive or non-executive capacity in such areas as commerce, industry, service, the Public sector, education, the not for profit sector, regulatory bodies or professional bodies, or a Chartered Accountant contracted by such entities.

Chartered Accountant in public practice: A Chartered Accountant, irrespective of functional classification (e.g., Audit, tax or consulting) in a firm that provides professional services. This term is also used to refer to a firm of Chartered Accountants in public practice

Clearly insignificant: A matter that is deemed to be both trivial and inconsequential.

Close family: A parent, child or sibling, who is an immediate family member.

Contingent fee: A fee calculated on a predetermined basis relating to the outcome or result of a transaction or the result of the work performed. A fee that is established by a court or other public authority is not a contingent fee.

Direct financial interest: A financial interest: owned directly by and under the control of an individual or entity (including those managed on a discretionary basis by others); or • Beneficially owned through a collective investment vehicle, estate, trust or other intermediary over which the individual or entity has control.

Director or Officer: Those charged with the governance of an entity, regardless of their title, which may vary from time to time. Discussion – means explanations and further clarification.

Engagement Partner: The partner or other person in the firm who is responsible for the engagement and its performance, and for the report that is issued on behalf of the firm, and who, where required, has the appropriate authority from a professional, legal or regulatory body.

Engagement quality control review: A process designed to provide an objective evaluation, before the report is issued, of the significant judgments the engagement team made and the conclusions they reached in formulating the report.

Engagement team: All personnel performing an engagement, including any experts contracted by the firm in connection with that engagement.

Existing accountant: A Chartered Accountant in public practice currently holding an audit appointment or carrying out accounting, taxation, consulting or similar professional services for a client.

Financial interest; An interest in an equity or other security, debenture, loan or other debt instrument of an entity, including rights and obligations to acquire such an interest and derivatives directly related to such interest. Financial statements: The balance sheets, income statements or profit and loss accounts, statements of changes in financial position (which may be presented in a variety of ways, for example, as a statement of cash flows or a statement of fund flows), notes and other statements and explanatory material which are identified as being part of the financial statements.

Financial statement audit client: An entity in respect of which a firm conducts a financial statement audit engagement. When the client is a listed entity, financial statement audit client will always include its related entities.

Financial statement audit engagement: A reasonable assurance engagement in which a Chartered Accountant in public practice expresses an opinion whether financial statements are prepared in all material respects in accordance with an identified financial reporting framework, such as an engagement conducted in accordance with International Standards on Auditing. This includes a Statutory Audit, which is a financial statement audit required by legislation or other regulation. Firm: (a) A sole practitioner, partnership or corporation of Chartered Accountants; (b) An entity that controls such parties; and (c) An entity controlled by such parties.

Financial Statements Audit Client – means a client who has retained a member to act as an external auditor as against carrying out other assurance agents e.g. value for money audit to the financial statement of the issuing firm.

Guidance- are further exposition of the subject matter in order to assist the Chartered Accountant to understand the fundamental Principles which is aimed at achieving best professional practices.

Infamous Conduct – means any act or omission, which by the standards of the Institute is shameful or disgraceful.

ICAN Act – is the Federal legislation with any amendments first known as Act of Parliament No. 15 of 1965 and subsequent re-enactments to regulate the profession of accountancy and for matters connected therewith.

Immediate family : A spouse (or equivalent) or dependant

Independence: Independence is:

(a) Independence of mind – the states of mind that permits the provision of an opinion without being affected by influences that compromise professional judgment, allowing an individual to act with integrity, and exercise objectivity and professional judgment. (b) Independence in appearance – the avoidance of facts and circumstances that are so significant a reasonable and informed third party, having knowledge of all relevant information, including any safeguards applied, would reasonably conclude a firm's, or a member of the assurance team's, integrity, objectivity or professional skepticism had been compromised.

Indirect financial interest: A financial interest beneficially owned through a collective investment vehicle, estate, trust or other intermediary over which the individual or entity has no control.

Letterhead – means any known format or design of which a member usually represents or intends to represent its name and address on its writing paper.

Misconduct – means any unlawful or improper or immoral behaviour; the failure, omission or violation of law or duty. Member – means any member of the Institute, and membership shall be construed accordingly.

Member firm – means: a) a member engaged in public practice as a sole practitioner; or b) a partnership engaged in public practice of which all the partners are member.

Network firm: An entity under common control, ownership or management with the firm or any entity that a reasonable and informed third party having knowledge of all relevant information would reasonably conclude as being part of the firm nationally or internationally.

Professional Misconduct – means any dishonest act or attempt to subvert the course of the accounting profession by use of deceptive or reprehensible methods, whether deliberate or not.

Procedure – means the formal steps for undertaking any process under the Rules

Procedures- are steps taken by Firms to ensure that threats to fundamental Principles are recognized, documented and mitigated. These might not be disclosed to outsiders unless the disciplinary or regulatory follow up requires it.

Professional services: Services requiring accountancy or related skills performed by a Chartered Accountant including accounting, auditing, taxation, Management consulting and financial management services.

Quoted Entity – means a listed company on any of the Stock Exchange. Listed entity: An entity whose shares, stock or debt are quoted or listed on a recognized stock exchange, or are marketed under the regulations of a recognized stock exchange or other equivalent body.

Related entity: An entity that has any of the following relationships with the client: (a) An entity that has direct or indirect control over the client provided the client is material to such entity; (b) An entity with a direct financial interest in the client provided that such entity has significant influence over the client and the interest in the client is material to such entity; (d) An entity over which the client has direct or indirect control; (e) An entity in which the client, or an entity related to the client under (c) Above has a direct financial interest that gives it significant influence over such entity and the interest is material to the client and its related entity in (c); and An entity which is under common control with the client (hereinafter a "sister entity") provided the sister entity and the client are both material to the entity that controls both the client and sister entity.

Statements – (or Financial Reports) are a record of a business' financial flows (revenues/expenses) and levels (assets/liabilities), including Income Statement, Balance Sheet, Cash flow Statement, Statements of changes in Shareholder equity, etc.

www.ingramcontent.com/pod-product-compliance
Lightning Source LLC
Chambersburg PA
CBHW060348200326
41519CB00011BA/2068